LEVERAGE YOUR TIME
BALANCE YOUR LIFE

also by John Ingram Walker, M.D.

books:

Leverage Your Time, Balance Your Life

50 Ways To Keep Your Lover

Jim Reid's Winning Basketball

The Best of the Self Help Books

A Life Well Lived

Everybody's Guide to Emotional Well-Being:
Helping Yourself Get Help

audiocassettes:

Total Self-Help: The Fundamental Principles of
Personal Growth

LEVERAGE YOUR TIME
BALANCE YOUR LIFE

John Ingram Walker, M.D.

Life Works Publishing Company

Published by:
    Life Works Publishing
    7967 Turf Paradise Lane
    Fair Oaks Ranch, Texas 78015
    (210) 698-2758
    Fax: (210) 698-9158

Copy Editors:
    Lynette Weaver, Wende Whitus

Cover Design:
    Paul Soupiset for Toolbox Studios

Printed and bound in the United States of America
        Print and Bind Direct!
        Books@printandbind.com

ISBN 0-9621073-5-2

4th Printing – March 2000

Dedication

To Victoria
Who balances time with the sweet fundamental things of life
and who, with gentle manner, makes a house a home.

Contents

Why I Wrote This Book

I wrote this book because most of us, almost all the time, fight the battle for possession and power. We find ourselves trapped on the freeway of rush. We have a shopping-mall mentality, a lunch hour McDonald's appetite, a sales-meeting life's philosophy. Before we know it, perhaps even without wanting to, we find ourselves leaping into the commotion without really considering whether we have an option. Our minds are made static by noise—radios bellowing, TVs babbling, pagers beeping, traffic buzzing. Everywhere, all the time, voices call our names. All of us are busy, perhaps productive...and very tired.

All of us sense that we were not made for the rush-hour, freeway kind of life we frenetically live. We seek calm, not chaos. We know, innately, that simpler times create better times. We desire peace, a life that focuses on beauty and truth, a life separate from the cluttered existence our culture promotes.

Yet, activity is necessary. We must produce-all of us-or we become drones of society, unweaned heifers sucking the public teat. Inactivity destroys the zest for life. There's no joy in constant watching, just numbed buttocks and deadened minds. We were not made to sit and isolate ourselves. We were created for motion and mastery.

Is there a half way point between burn out and rust out? Yes. Balance is a choice.

Each day we can find a place to retreat. We can turn off our noise boxes and enjoy a refuge where we can rest and renew. We can eliminate non-productive activities. We can say "no." We can reserve a corner of peace, close our eyes and step through our mind's windows into a simpler world. We can enjoy a book. Stroll down a forest's path.

The sweet fundamental things of life make living worthwhile. Life is balanced by being alive to both sides of our nature–duty and serenity, work and love, activity and rest.

Nearly all of us blame our unbalanced life on the lack of time. We can be heard complaining in the elevator, in the office, in the grocery store, at church, at home, at the gym. We proclaim our dear time's loss. We marvel at time's swift foot. We recognize ourselves in these cries:

"I'm in the car all day and night taking the kids from one event to another."

"Too many projects!"

"Family? I never have enough time for them."

"The little things consume the time I could dedicate to important activities."

"I get a headache every time the phone rings."

"All those business meetings do for me is put callouses on my rear end."

"These constant interruptions make me sick to the stomach."

"We didn't take a vacation last year because our business consumed us."

"Time for myself? You've got to be kidding!"

"Committee meeting!?! Oh no!!! Not another one!!!"

"Life style? What's that?"

"A nap? Considered it....But no time for one."

"Spiritual life? Oh yes, I attend church for an hour just about every Sunday."

"I could have 48 hours a day and still couldn't catch up."

Poor time management, not lack of time, engenders these complaints. Poor planning steals hours each day at home, at work, from the mother, the student, the teacher, the doctor, the lawyer...even the candlestick maker. This book was written for all of us—to help us enjoy a productive life, a balanced life, a successful, meaningful life—and to find time for every activity worthwhile...time for every season under the sun.

Haven't many books been written on time management? Yes...hundreds rest on dusty shelves. Either they haven't been read or they haven't been understood. They are too impractical or too long. The more books that have been churned out, the less time we have to study them and practice the techniques suggested in them.

That's what makes *Leverage Your Time, Balance Your Life* unique. It's brief. To the point. Gives clear suggestions. Can be read in one night. Referred to during the day. It can be read again and again, until every page becomes implanted in the mind. *Leverage Your Time, Balance Your Life* is a handbook. A handbook for living.

I wrote this book in the second person because it's designed for you. You are busy. You don't have time—yet—for theory or romantic prose or stories. You just want the facts. Cut to the heart of the thing. Get on with it.

Applying what's written in *Leverage Your Time, Balance Your Life* will give you a fulfilled life, a balanced life. Practicing what's written here will help you:

- Have time for your dreams to come true
- Find time you never knew you had
- Learn to set priorities
- Organize your life
- Learn to refuse worthless projects
- Defeat procrastination
- Organize efficient time-saving meetings
- Give up the quest for perfection
- Overcome indecisiveness
- Balance your work and leisure time
- Find time for romance
- Cultivate a spiritual life that gives life meaning
- Have fun every day
- Use rest power
- Improve family communication
- Find time for your children
- Rid your life of time wasters
- Write bold, brief, empowering letters and memos
- Defeat negative emotions that mess up your life
- Rid yourself of bad habits that steal your time
- Add more life to your years
- Live one day at a time
- Reduce paperwork clutter
- Translate your dreams into achievable goals
- Know your core values for a successful life

Time to Dream

The Bigger the Dream, the More the Time

Whatever you can do or dream you can begin it.
Boldness has genius, power and magic to it.
                                        -- Goethe

*W*ho stole the American dream?

Who snatched our aspiration to be in charge of our lives? Who hampered our desire to go as far and as high as our spirit and character could take us? The government? Corporate America? Our boss? Our friends? Our family? Television? Laziness? Procrastination? Disorganization? Low self-esteem?

Some may have forgotten how to dream—or never learned. Others may just watch visionaries build their dreams—and think it's impossible to have what they have. A few people walk around saying, *"What's happening? Who's dreaming?"*

We surrender our dreams for many reasons. Whatever the cause—social or psychological—a meager number of people know how to dream big. That's sad, because we limit our potential when we won't allow ourselves to dream. No matter who (or what) caused us to relinquish our dreams, we—each of us—have the ultimate responsibility for deciding to dream again. Our desire determines our destiny.

All of us would do well to open our minds to our dreams—and to expand our dreams.

Why? Because the bountiful dreamers, and those who plan and organize their dreams, have a life of abundance.

They are fulfilled. Productive. Enthusiastic. Energetic dreamers look forward to each new day. Dream builders have all the money they want to help others. They contribute to society and savor the fruits of their labor. They have time to enjoy life. Time and money give them lifestyle—the freedom to take vacations whenever they want, the opportunity to choose how to live their lives, the privilege to raise a family without restraint, and the capacity to develop their talents.

Prodigious dreamers have the greatest motivation to plan and organize their lives to fulfill their dreams. Message: Dream liberally! Dream lavishly! Dream luxuriantly!

If you've lost your dream, resolve to change now. Expand your vision. Open your mind to unlimited possibilities. Learn to dream again. Success and fulfillment always begin with desire.

Build Your Own Dream

You can start to dream with a vision statement—a phrase or sentence that tells what you are about. Here's an example of a vision statement: "I live a life that will bring encouragement, optimism and hope to all I meet." Note that the statement is in the first person, present tense indicating that the future begins now.

As you consider your vision statement, be certain you're using your own measuring stick—not your mother's, or father's, or your wife's, or your husband's, or your friend's. What do you want out of life? What's important to you? What are you about?

Here are some questions to help define your vision statement. As you answer these questions you'll be able to understand what motivates you:

What three activities are most important to you?

1._____

2._____

3._____

What three activities give you the most enjoyment?

1._____

2._____

3._____

What three things do you want written on your tombstone?

1._____

2._____

3._____

What three things do you want to do for others?

1._____

2._____

3._____

What three things would you change about your life?

1._____

2._____

3._____

What three qualities would you most like to see associated with your reputation?

1._____

2._____

3._____

Expand Your Financial Dreams.

What ten things do you want in life? Would you like to get out of debt? What kind of house do you want? What kind of cars do you want to drive? If you had all the money you wanted, where would you go on a vacation? Where do you want your children to go to college? How much money would you like to give to your church or to charities? When do you want to retire? (Retirement depends on money, not age.) What net worth do you want to accumulate?

Make a dream list here:

1._____
2._____
3._____
4._____
5._____
6._____
7._____
8._____
9._____
10._____

Now study everything you have written so far. Sum-up, in one or two sentences, a concise description of who you want to be. Write your vision statement in the first person, present tense.

I am a person who: _____

_____

_____

_____

_____

Formulating a vision statement and writing down those things you desire helps you focus on your pleasures, your talents, and your bliss. Once you've expanded your vision, your expectations will direct you toward fulfilling your dreams.

It helps to put your dream statement on the refrigerator. Read it regularly. Cut out pictures of the things you want to enjoy. Look at the pictures several times a day. See yourself becoming your dream and living the life you want to live.

When you dream extraordinary dreams, some people—perhaps a family member, friend, co-worker, or even your boss—may try to take your vision from you. When they see pictures of your dreams on the refrigerator or the bathroom mirror, they will think you have flipped. When they see a first person, present tense, vision statement they will know you have gone over the edge. When they see you joyful and smiling, positive and optimistic, they'll wonder what drug you are taking.

They will worry about you. They will try to steal your dream: *"Don't get so excited, this might not work out." "You've got a good job; why do you want to change to something so uncertain?" "I know someone who tried that and they failed miserably."*

Unfulfilled people are like crabs. Put crabs in a bucket and watch. If one crab attempts to crawl out of a bucket, the others pull the adventurer back down. People are like that. If you get a dream, they'll try to destroy it.

Go for excellence and you'll be laughed at, criticized, and gossiped about. Who cares? It's your life. Trade acceptance for excellence.

When someone or some event in your life begins to steal your dream, don't despair. Stand tall and straight, face the cold and penetrating wind of dissension and press on toward your dream.

Setting Goals To Achieve Your Dreams

A dream without a goal is similar to taking an automobile trip without a road map. You will surely arrive, but where? To make certain that you achieve your dreams set specific, measurable goals that are compatible with your dreams.

Break goals down into small steps, review them daily and revise them regularly. List activities that will help you attain your goals. Develop a detailed, scheduled plan of action, then take one small step at a time to move toward your goals.

Henry David Thoreau said, *"If one marches confidently in the direction of his dreams and endeavors to lead the life he has imagined, he will meet with success unexpected in common hours."*

You can strengthen the belief that your goals will be reached by acting as if they have already been met.

Speak, think, act, and live the traits and qualities you desire. You then become that person.

In establishing goals, keep these guidelines in mind:

- Goals should be for you and not for someone else.

- Goals should be realistic and believable.

- Goals must be achievable, so attack big goals in short steps, one at a time. For example, to lose 50 pounds, establish a goal to lose one pound a week for 50 weeks.

- Goals should allow you to enjoy life. Don't tackle so much work that you don't have enough time to relax. The purpose of goal setting is to reduce, not increase frustration.

Follow these steps in making your goals useful:

- Write your goals on a single sheet of paper.

- Read your goals every day.

- Each day question your resolve: *"Am I doing those things that will help me achieve my goals?"*

And remember:

- Unwritten goals are simply wishes.

- Successful achievement depends on commitment to your goal. Review reinforces commitment.

- Asking yourself the activity question—*"Am I doing those things that I need to do to achieve my goals?"*—will help focus your energy.

- As you change, change your goals.

Types of Goals

Family, Spiritual and Personal Goals

List the objectives you want to achieve outside your career in this section. Remember, as with all goals, being specific helps manage your time:

- How much time do you want to spend with your family?

- How do you want to spend your time with your family?
- How do you want to spend your leisure time?
- How many hours do you want to spend relaxing?
- How much time do you want to spend in specific spiritual pursuits?

My personal, family, and spiritual goals are:

1._____

2._____

3._____

Career Goals

Career success requires a game plan and persistence. We can achieve whatever we work steadily and persistently to accomplish. Most of us spend time on career wishes because we fail to make and write down specific plans for our professional life. Or we write career goals mandated by our company. What are your goals for your career? Be specific.

- How do you want to advance your career in the next twelve months?
- What do you want to accomplish in the next 5 years?
- What are your lifetime career goals?

My career goals are:

1._____

2._____

3._____

Self-Improvement Goals

Success in life depends on a steady pursuit of self-improvement. Here are some suggestions for self-improvement goals:

- Read books that improve your attitude and people skills for fifteen minutes every night. Reading just before you go to sleep allows the words to sink into your unconscious. Reading positive literature daily helps dilute the negative in your life.

- Listen to educational cassettes or disks when you are driving in your car. If for four years, you listen to educational tapes every time you get in your car you will have the equivalent of a college education.

- Join Toastmasters to set your words—and your career—on fire.

- Learn a foreign language.

My self-improvement goals are:

1._____

2._____

3._____

Activity List

To achieve your goals, act. Act now! Without action, your dreams are worthless. Your goals are wishes. Your plans are ashes. Action alone gives worth to your dreams. Only action determines your value. You are what you do. Your actions describe you.

The lazy wait until tomorrow. The weak expect to be strong tomorrow. The failure anticipates success tomorrow. Success does not linger. Act now! Act now!. Act now! Today is the perfect day to begin.

Plug away at the daily activities that fulfill your dreams. Through self-discipline—developing the habit of doing the best you can day after day—you gain the maximum benefits from your time. Cultivating a strong, healthy routine supports a successful, fulfilled life.

Your activities become habits. Habits become your character. Your character becomes your destiny. Become a slave to good habits. Doing the right things right, minute by minute, hour by hour, day by day develops strength of character that leads to success after success.

Routine activities develop habits that will help you achieve your goals and your dreams. If your goal is to write a book in one year, one of your daily activities would be to write a page a day.

If you wanted to make a million dollars in annual sales, one of your activities may consist of making ten sales calls daily.

Focus your activities on those things that will help you achieve your goals. Make a list of activities that you will do daily or weekly to accomplish your goals and do them—every day, every week, every year. Your daily activities can be divided into personal, family, and spiritual activities; career activities; and self improvement activities.

My personal, family, and spiritual activities are:

1._____

2._____

3._____

My career activities are:

1._____

2._____

3._____

My self-improvement goals are:

1._____

2._____

3._____

Summary

Keeping your eyes on your dream will make your goals, activities, and habits enjoyable. Just as a champion bull rider concentrates on completing an eight second ride, a football player focuses on each five second play, and an alcoholic remains sober one day at a time, you—the self-disciplined achiever—give your best effort to each activity. Failure to visualize a clear future objective—failure to keep your eyes focused on your dreams—makes meaningful routine dull and boring.

When you become frustrated by the routine, keep your eyes on the dream.

When you become disappointed by rejection, remember the dream.

When you fail to advance as quickly as you would like, visualize accomplishing your dream.

Hear what people will say when you attain your dream. See what people will do when your dreams come true. Feel—right now—the excitement of fulfilling your dream. Keep your dream—and the exhilaration of completing your dream—in your heart and mind all the time.

From dreams, come goals.
From goals, come activities.
From activities, come routines.
From routines, come habits.
From habits, come character.

Character is marked by the following virtues: *integrity, persistence, courage, love, joy, peace, patience, kindness, goodness, faithfulness, gentleness, self-control, and wisdom.*

These virtues guarantee that your dreams—your incredible dreams—will be fulfilled.

Time for Priorities

Neglecting the Unimportant

*Those who apply themselves too closely to little things
often become incapable of great things.*
-- LaRochefoucauld

*h*uge dreams are worthless without the time to make them come true.

Many of us complain that we don't have enough time. *False!* All of us have the time. Instead, most of us waste the time we have. Or because we don't think that we can achieve our fabulous dreams, we won't set aside time to fulfill them. We spend all our time on insignificant things and have no time left for the activities that will achieve our dreams. We're too busy making a living to develop a lifestyle. That's what this chapter is about—efficiency and productivity—making dreams a reality.

First Things First

A well-used time management rule says, *"Success depends on what you neglect."* To get something important accomplished, neglect the unimportant, devote time to the important.

Always follow the cardinal rule of time management: First things first. Early each morning make a list of those things to be accomplished. Review your goals. Then number your activities in the order of their importance based on how those activities will help you accomplish your goals. Complete the first item first. The second, second. The third, third. If you don't get to number four, no big deal. Avoid criticizing yourself if you fail to achieve everything on your list. Remember, you did the most important things first.

Remember the 80/20 Rule

The 80/20 rule comes from Pareto, an Italian economist, who found that:

- 80% of the wealth is held by 20% of the people.
- 80% of the sales are made by 20% of the sales force.
- 80% of the purchases are made by 20% of the customers.
- 80% of books borrowed from libraries are borrowed by 20% of the people.
- 80% of the money made in seminars will be with 20% of the companies.
- 80% of the work completed will be done by 20% of the people.

Focus eighty percent of your energy on 20% of the people and activities that pay big dividends.

Overcome Procrastination

Procrastination, doing low-priority tasks before high priority activities, robs us of valuable time. We usually do the least important things first because they are easier. We put off the most important things because they are hardier. When we work on the unimportant, we worry about the crucial tasks that aren't getting done. We get tension headaches. Ulcers. High blood pressure. Our doctors get rich, but we still haven't done what's most important. There are four major reasons for procrastination:

1. Laziness

To defeat laziness, begin. Once moving, you'll tend to keep going. It takes greater energy to start an activity than to sustain it. For example, if you're writing a screen play, put something on paper. Forget about sharpening pencils, arranging paper, reading one more script for inspiration. Write. Writers write.

2. *The Quest for Perfection*

Nobody is perfect. Nothing created by anybody is perfect. Stop fretting about getting everything just right. Learn to do your best and accept the results. Expecting perfection never gets anything accomplished. To continue with the writing analogy, get that first draft done. Forget semicolons, active verbs, dangling participles, mixed metaphors. Just get something down on paper. You can revise and rewrite the screenplay later.

3. *Indecisiveness*

To overcome indecisiveness, use the ready, fire, aim approach. Fire it up there. Then aim it. Make some mistakes. Learn. Adjust. Move on.

4. *Difficult Tasks*

Break down a difficult task into easy steps. Just do a little at a time. You write a screenplay or a book one page at a time. Write one page a day and at the end of a year you will have written 365 pages.

Saying "No" to Make Your Dreams Come True

Many of us have difficulty saying *"no."* We give, give, give until our time and energy have been consumed, dedicating our selves to martyrdom. Hours are wasted saying "yes" to projects that don't hold our interest.

Wasting time volunteering for activities that are less important than accomplishing our goals causes resentment and irritability. We must say "no" immediately to projects that interfere with our goals. The sooner we get in the habit of managing our time, the quicker we can accomplish the goals that matter. Remember: If we don't control our allotment of time, someone else will.

Most commonly we say *"yes"* in an attempt to have people like us. We're like puppy dogs wagging our tails at everyone we meet, pleading for them to be our friends.

At other times guilt causes us to say *"yes"* to projects that don't help us accomplish our goals. We sigh deeply and with a droopy face say: *"Well, someone has to participate in the project. It might as well be me."*

After we've said *"yes,"* we might spend countless hours trying to get out of our commitment. Or we might do a sloppy job on projects that we don't enjoy. This behavior annoys and disappoints others. Saying *"no"* immediately—and with respect—saves everyone a great deal of frustration.

Is saying *"no"* to less important projects selfish? Of course not! If our values are correct, conserving time for our goals will eventually help more people than a project that fails to fulfill our dreams.

Practice saying *"no"* with grace. You can learn to let your "no" make the other person feel important. Here are couple of honest ways to say *"no"* with style:

"Wow! That's a worthwhile project. It doesn't fit into my time schedule right now. I'm honored that you would ask me to participate as a committee member. Thanks for asking. Unfortunately, because of other time pressing commitments, I'll have to decline. No. (Pause for a second or two.) *I wish you well. Good-bye."*

"That project sounds great. I bet you will do well on it. You've got a lot of drive and ambition. Unfortunately, I don't have the talent or commitment to participate. One of the things I've learned through the years is what I can and can't do. My getting involved would be a waste of your time. No. (Pause for a second or two.) *Best wishes on your project. Good bye."*

When you say *"no"* with refinement you make the other person feel important. You show respect to the other person. And you treat yourself with respect. You are essentially saying to yourself, *"I have dreams and goals. I know the things I want and I'm going after them."*

Remember: It's better to be respected than liked. When others respect you, they will eventually begin to like you for your strength of character.

Listen to Save Time

Have you been late for a meeting because you didn't listen carefully to directions? Have you gotten the wrong impression about a business deal so time was wasted putting together a project that no one wanted? Have you spent hours trying to restore harmony after a misunderstanding offended your spouse? Has a misinterpretation of what you thought you heard caused a loss of time with your children, friends or associates?

Listening is a lost art ... and an art that can be learned. Mastered and used appropriately, proper listening can allow you to save valuable hours per week. Listening will help you make time-saving decisions. You'll become a brilliant conversationalist. You'll be popular. Respected.

Why does a good listener acquire more affection than a good talker? Because a good listener always allows people to hear their favorite speakers—themselves. People are a thousand times more likely to be interested in themselves than in you.

Here are the cardinal techniques for listening:

- Make the other person feel important by using *"you"* words.

- Observe the person who is talking.

- Lean toward the speaker and listen intently.

- Don't interrupt with long *"I"* statements.

- Ask questions.

- Reflect back using the speaker's words.

Simple rules? Yes. But not commonly practiced. Think about it. When you last communicated with your family, were you looking at them or at the television? When listening to a report, were you focused on the speaker?

Listening begins and ends with making the other person feel important. Listen more, talk less. To listen, replace *"I,"* *"me,"* *"my,"* and *"mine"* with *"you"* and *"yours."* The more the *"you"* word is used, the more important people feel. The more important they feel, the better and quicker they respond.

Eye contact—looking at the speaker—is crucial. Because the eyes are the gateway to the soul, communication at the deepest level comes from eye contact.

Concentrating on the speaker builds trust. Improves rapport. Enhances hearing. You pick-up nuances in facial expression and body posture when you watch the speaker.

Leaning toward the speaker reflects interest. An open, interested posture encourages the speaker and builds confidence in the relationship. Leaning away indicates indifference.

Interrupting with I statements wastes time. Avoid comments such as, *"I lived in Georgetown once...;" "Did you know I...;"* or *"I felt like that before...; I remember...."*

Interrupting with clarifying or empathetic queries encourages the person to get to the point. The following interruptions help speed the person along: *"I understand....What happened next?"* or *"I know how you feel....After that what happened?"* or *"Would you please clarify that? Did that happen before or after...."*

Asking questions develops rapport and understanding. When people enjoy being with you, they share important matters. Talking to people about themselves works with human nature. Talking about yourself works against human nature.

Questions lead to the royal path of persuasion. Asking questions will tell you what others want, what motivates them. You can then use this knowledge to develop a time saving win-win situation. By helping other people get what they want, you can get what you want.

Respect Your Time and the Time Of Others: Be Brief

Brevity, the heart of conversation, shows respect. Treating the other person with respect encourages productive conferences and meetings. Smile. Nod affirmatively. Look the person in the eye. Don't appear to be in a hurry. Say, "Because we respect each other's time, let's briefly cover the main topics and we'll decide what to do about them." Stand up—politely—when you are ready to terminate the conversation.

Courtesty Improves Scheduled Appointments

Always be on time. It's polite.

Always be on time. It's the right thing to do.

Always be on time. It saves time.

Always leave before your time is up. It's respectful.

What if people make you wait longer than is usually expected? Let them know that your time is just as valuable as theirs. Courteously say: *"Mr. Banker, your time is valuable and it seems as if you have had a hectic day. I know how you feel, I've had days like that before, too. I have a meeting that starts in an hour; I'm afraid that I won't be able to discuss my account with you and get to that meeting on time. Loan me the $1 million now and we'll both save time."* A statement like this tells Mr. Banker that you value your time as much as he does his. Next time you have an appointment, you will be seen promptly. If not, find a more respectful banker—and one who has money to loan.

Avoid Boring Conversations

Time is too precious to be bored. Learn something from everyone you meet. Everyone has an interesting story. If listless conversations or people frustrate you, move on. Seek more interesting friends and associates. Avoid tedium.

Decrease Interruptions

Establish certain periods during the day to accept and return phone calls. Close your door when you are trying to get something done. Set limits at the beginning of visits.

Tip In Advance

If you want prompt service in a busy restaurant, give the tip before the meal is served. After all, the word "tip" was originally an acronym for "To Insure Performance." If you want to insure performance, try giving the tip first. You'll be amazed how quickly and courteously you'll be served.

Find Time You Never Knew You Had: Reduce Paperwork

• Clearing your cluttered desk will help bring order to your life. If your desk is a mess, resolve to clean it. Pending files, tickler files, and the trash will take care of the majority of papers that clutter your desk.

• Make an effort to handle every piece of paper only once. Respond to a letter while the letter is in front of you. Throw away low priority paperwork and junk mail.

• Keep your desk clear of all material except what you are working on at that moment. This technique prevents distraction and hopping from one project to the next.

Get Up Early

Most, but not all, successful people get up early. They leap from their beds and get the most important work done before the sun rises.

If meetings and routine work duties prevent you from accomplishing priority tasks, get an early start. Begin—and finish—your most essential work before everyone else arrives and the telephone starts ringing.

Sleep Less

Reducing your sleep time by 30 minutes each day will give you 7-1/2 extra days a year.

Remember, however, that each individual has a unique demand for sleep. The average sleep requirement for a young, healthy adult is just a few minutes under eight hours. As we age, we require less sleep.

Know Your Rhythms

Determine your most productive time and reserve it for prime projects. Don't spend your best hours on routine tasks such as answering mail and reading reports.

Win

Ask: *"What's the best use of my time right now?"*

This priority question will allow you to **WIN** (**W**hat's **I**mportant **N**ow) the time management battle.

Delegate

Certain tasks can be done by others. Delegate mechanical tasks and you will have more time to do those things others can't do.

Use Transistion Time Wisely

• Dictate messages and letters during travel time.

• Keep a book with you wherever you go. If you get stuck in rush hour traffic or if you are in an empty waiting room, remember this magic move: Pull out your book and start reading.

• Maximize your travel time by listening to educational audiocassette tapes.

Turn Off the Television

Throw your television away! Ninety-five percent of television is negative. Who needs more negative in their lives? Television robs more people of their valuable time then any instrument ever invented. Don't worry about keeping up with the news. If there's a nuclear war someone will let you know about it.

Although scrapping the television would be better than constantly watching mind constricting programs, there must be some balance in our television time. Television, a marvelous invention that could be used for improving and inspiring us, has become a terrible influence on our children and suggestible adults. Unwise choices in program selection can erode our minds and waste our time. Let us all—everyone of us—break the habit of flipping on the set when we walk in the room...and let us monitor what we watch.

Rest and Relax

Relaxing, a good use of time, saves energy and improves concentration, enabling you to get more done faster. Rest and think a few minutes before and after meetings. Break up your work schedule with a 10 minute respite every 90 minutes. Walk and/or nap 30 minutes each day. Avoid work on Sundays. A lumberjack knows that the oak cuts faster when he takes time to sharpen the ax.

Summary

Success requires time management. Using your time well will give you more time for living.

You'll add more time to your life and more life to your time.

Remember:

- Take care of first things first.
- Follow the 80/20 rule: spend 80% of your time with the top 20%.
- Begin now.
- Say *"no"* to the unimportant.
- **WIN: W**hat's **I**mportant **N**ow—the time management game.
- Use transition time appropriately.
- Handle every piece of paper one time only.
- Set limits on interruptions.
- Use your most productive time on prime projects.
- Listen carefully.
- Delegate.
- Take time to rest.

Time for Positive Living

Choosing Happiness

Attitudes are more important than facts.
-- Karl Menninger, M.D.

*P*oor emotional health robs us of valuable time and prevents us from enjoying a balanced life.

The good news: our emotional health depends on our attitude. We can choose: To accept or refuse love; grow from or surrender to challenges; enjoy or complain about our work; modify our habits or let our habits modify us; cultivate tranquility or be overwhelmed by stress; seize opportunities or cower in a corner; enjoy being alive or dread waking up. Proper attitudes create a life worth living and make time worthwhile.

Our response to life's difficulties determines our happiness and health. Within us resides the gift to accept responsibility for our own bliss. We can shape adversity into an advantage. We can turn tragedy into hope. We can live the life we choose. The power to change gives us the opportunity for a blessed and balanced life.

Feelings Come From Thoughts

The blind poet, Milton, wrote, *"The mind is its own place, and in itself can make a heaven of hell, a hell of heaven."*

Thoughts of two famous people underscore Milton's point:

Napoleon who had power, riches, and glory said, *"I have never known six happy days in my life."*

Helen Keller, rendered blind and deaf from childhood meningitis, declared, *"I have found life so beautiful."*

Events and acquisitions fail to give us joy. Our thoughts can. Mind-body research, psychoneuroimmunology, proves that negative thoughts produce stress hormones. Optimistic thoughts cause the release of endorphins and other beneficial brain chemicals causing good feelings. What we think determines how we feel.

Speak the Negative Away

Never verbalize a negative. We avoid saying anything negative about ourselves, our family, our friends, our career—about anything. Why? Because our words are like seeds. What we sow, we reap. Talk negative, reap negative.

Our mind is like a computer with a keyboard and a storage disk. Our senses represent our keyboard. Chemical pathways in the brain's unconscious represent the brain's storage disks. Anything that is typed into our keyboard will be stored for life. Our lips are part of our keyboard. Our lips program us. Speak negative and we program negative into our storage disk called the unconscious mind.

The storage disk (the unconscious mind) is unable to distinguish the truth from a lie. The unconscious believes everything that is put into it. As computer programmers say, *"Garbage In, Garbage Out."* Negative program, negative life.

Emile Coué, the pioneer of autosuggestion, coined the phrase:

"Day by day, in every way, I'm getting better and better. I feel healthy. I feel happy. I feel terrific."

He asked patients to repeat this phrase throughout the day. Those who followed his suggestion improved.

Words are a tremendous energy source. Negative words induce negative results; positive words produce positive results.

Negative speech undermines our health and our happiness. A secretary says, *"This computer is a pain in the neck"*—and guess who has a headache a few hours later? A tennis player says, *"I choke on the big points"*— and guess who loses important matches? A parent says, *"Our kids always get sick on vacation"*—and guess whose holiday is ruined?

How often have we heard ourselves say these words: *"I'm not as smart as everyone else." "I'm just unlucky." "I can't lose weight." "I'm not getting any younger." "I'm not as sharp as I used to be." "I'll never be a success." "I never have enough time." "I'm messy.""I'm disorganized." "Mondays depress me."*

As children we hear negative. When we watch television we see and hear negative. (The auditory and visual aspects of television make it a powerful programmer.) Our friends talk negatively. So we get in the habit. We begin to talk negatively. The more we hear ourselves talk, the more negative we speak. We verbalize the negative and our lives become negative. The more negative our lives become, the more we speak negative.

Check yourself. Listen consciously to everything you verbalize. Does most of your self-talk build you up or put you down? Would you type the words you say about yourself into your computer as lifelong directives?

Imagine getting on an airplane that contains the wrong program. Would you fly on that plane? Of course not. The program determines the plane's altitude, speed, course, and destination. An airplane with the wrong program will crash. When you hear yourself speak negatively—stop. Get on the right course. Speak positive words that guide you to success.

You can reprogram your brain. The chemical pathways in your brain's unconscious can be broken down in about twenty-one days. Replace negative words with positive words and the negative chemical pathways— the negative programs—will be destroyed in twenty-one days.

Once the negative programs are destroyed, more positive things will begin to happen. You will be on the flight path of success.

If words are the most powerful destiny shaper that we control—and they are—then by governing the words that come out of our mouths, we can have a better chance of having a fulfilled life.

Learn to see something positive in everything that happens. Speak hopeful words. Never miss an opportunity to praise others. Find and speak the good in every situation. Show appreciation at every opportunity. Encourage the timid. Fortify the weak. Use positive words to become all you can be and to help others to get the most out of life. Positive words give you confidence and, in turn, encourage others.

Rather than speaking the negative in advance, speak what you want as if your desire has already happened. Avoid speaking a negative future: *"We are looking forward to our vacation, but the first day we go on a trip the kids always get sick."* Guess what happens? Your children are sick the first day of your vacation. Speak positively about the future: *"We are looking forward to our vacation and this time the kids are going to be healthy the entire trip."* Your children have a much better chance of being healthy this time.

Positive speech is not designed to detract from your faith. Positive talk enhances your faith. Read the Bible. All of God's courageous leaders spoke positively—especially about the future.

The Power of Optimism

A fishing guide once said that catching a trout depends more on who's holding the pole than the bait that's on the hook. *"Optimists catch more fish,"* he said. *"They believe they're going to catch 'em and they catch 'em."*

Actor Tommy Lee Jones said, *"I work on being optimistic about life. Pessimism, certainly cynicism, is an enemy. Those things destroy possibilities. Optimism is the right outlook to have. I'm convinced it creates possibilities."*

On or in mountain streams, on the movie set, and in controlled laboratories optimists do better. Empirical findings and scientific studies indicate that optimists are more successful in all aspects of life than pessimists. Because optimists are more resilient, they turn defeat into victory.

Optimism helps athletes. Swimmers were given a psychological test that measured attitude. Those who scored high on optimism performed better after a defeat. Swimmers who scored low on optimism performed worse after a defeat.

Optimism helps students. Psychologists gave college freshmen tests to measure optimism. Four years later, the psychologists found that optimism predicted grades better than SAT scores or high-school grades.

Optimism helps sales people. About three quarters of insurance salesmen quit in their first three years. Guess what? Pessimists quit twice as often as optimists. Optimistic insurance sales people sell almost forty percent more insurance than pessimists sell.

MetLife Insurance executives hired a special group of applicants who failed the normal screening tests, but scored high on optimism. The first year on the job the *"dumb"* optimists sold 21% more insurance than the *"smart"* pessimists. The second year, the optimists sold 57% more insurance than the pessimists. *"Dumb"* optimists sell more insurance than "smart" pessimists.

Optimism can be learned! Increase your belief in several areas of your life:

- Believe in a God who gives you peace and joy.

- Believe in a country that gives you the freedom to develop your talents.

- Believe in a free-enterprise system that provides you a method to succeed.

- Believe in you.

- Believe in positive action.

Nothing builds optimism more than action. Act and learn from your actions. Succeed by taking little baby steps toward success. Each successful attempt teaches you how to improve. Your optimism soars every time you improve on what you learn.

Attitude is Everything

Two shoe salesmen were given a new territory on a Pacific island. Immediately upon arrival, the first sales-man placed an urgent call to the home office: *"Get me out of here. No one on this island wears shoes."*

The second salesman sent an e-mail request to the factory, *"Please put everybody on overtime. Will need as many shoes as you can manufacture. No one on this island has any shoes."*

Attitude determines the difference between shoed or shoeless. Attitude is more critical than events. It's more significant than what's happened or what's hap-pening. Attitude is more consequential than the past, than genetics, than education, than money. Attitude is more important than what other people think...or say...or do. It is more important than appearance or tal-ent. Attitude will make or break an individual, a home, a company, or a country.

Because attitude determines whether we are happy or unhappy, fulfilled or empty, the positive perspective assures us that we can never fail. A hopeful attitude guarantees internal success. Attitude—the altitude adjuster—determines whether we fly high or low, crash or soar, glide or slide.

A couple of days ago I had a pity party. I became upset with everything and everybody. Suddenly I felt ashamed. I wasn't any better than a spoilsport. I rebuked myself: *"Anybody can have a positive attitude when things are going well. It's how you act when things are going badly that determines the strength of your character. An appropriate attitude means feeling hopeful in challenging times. Stop feeling sorry for yourself. Count your blessings. Look for the good."*

I shared my insight with a friend who, later that day, gave me a adhesive label to place on my bathroom mirror. Now whenever I shave, brush my teeth, or comb my hair, I see the message: ***Attitude is Everything.*** This little reminder helps me tidy up my point of view.

Whether we are running hot, running cold, or simply running on overload, we can take charge of our attitude by remembering these aphorisms:

- Success has more to do with our emotional disposition than with our social position.

- Kites rise against the wind, not with it.

- A rubber band becomes effective only when it's stretched.

- More opportunities exist than there are people willing to seize them.

- What matters is what happens in us not to us.

- You can tell when you are on the road to success. It's uphill all the way.

- When Goliath appeared, David said, *"He's so big I can't miss."*

- Wait until the lows pass and you will feel on top of things.

- Choices, not circumstances, determine how we think.

- Because action cures misery change your motion to create positive emotion.

- Where there is no faith in the future, there is no power in the present.

- To accept failure as final is to be finally a failure.

- Failure is the line of least persistence.

- Others can stop us temporarily, but we are the only ones who can stop ourselves permanently.

- Our lips program our brain for success or failure.

- Act "as if" we are successful and we will be.

- Attitude determines whether our failures make us or break us.

- Life is one percent what happens to us and 99 percent how we react to what happens.

- Gratitude adjusts our attitude.

Do platitudes help us live better? Do bathroom decals influence us? Are positive stories helpful? You bet! Suggestions–both positive and negative–powerfully influence our attitudes. Here's an example:

A psychologist stood in the produce department of a grocery store. As each customer passed him, the psychologist tested their reaction to verbal influence. He declared to one group, *"You don't like strawberries do you?"* 90% of the customers agreed with his statement.

He offered the next group a basket of strawberries with this assertive query, *"You want some strawberries, don't you?!"* Half of them accepted his strawberries.

He asked the third group, *"Do you want one or two baskets of strawberries?"* 40% of these customers took two baskets; 50% took one basket; and only 10% took no strawberries.

What is said to us and what we say to ourselves strongly impacts our attitude about everything we encounter—from shoes to strawberries. So tape those aphorisms to your refrigerator door....And, by the way, have you heard? Strawberry-colored shoes are hot items this season.

Choose Enthusiasm

Enthusiasm. Corporate presidents voted it the most valuable personality trait. It's the biggest single factor in successful selling. It wins ball games. Inspires audiences. Enhances learning. Builds team spirit. Propels careers. Makes dull days bright.

Choose enthusiasm by seeing your dreams come true. Think enthusiastically. Talk enthusiastically. Become enthusiastic by acting enthusiastic. Your thoughts and actions determine your level of enthusiasm.

Add Zip to Everything You Do

Walk fast. Put a bounce in your step. A vigorous, hearty handshake indicates you are glad to be alive and happy to be with the other person. A robust smile radiates enthusiasm. Reply to the mundane, *"How do you do?"* with an attention getting, *"Fantastic...and I'm going to get better!"* Put spirit into your speech by varying the pace, raising and lowering the pitch, changing the tone and modulation. Talk with more than your mouth—use wide sweeping gestures. Don't hold back. Turn it on. Force yourself to act with enthusiasim, and soon you will feel enthusiastic.

This is the era of dramatization. Simply stating the facts isn't enough. The truth must be made vibrant, arresting, theatrical. If you want to keep and hold someone's attention, you must use showmanship.

Broadcast Good News

No one ever made a friend or accomplished anything worthwhile by transmitting bad news. Good news, on the other hand, promotes good will and spreads enthusiasm. The message, *"I've got good news"* gets the attention of everyone. Take sunshine to work. Talk about the positive things your company is doing. Compliment people you work with. Let them know you have faith in them. Always aim to make the person you talk to feel better than he otherwise would.

Talk to your family about the amusing, pleasant things you experienced during the day and let the disagreeable stay concealed. Bring rainbows home. If you can't say anything good about your physical health say nothing at all. No one wants to hear about your aches and problems. Instead, glorify in your good health and the good things that are happening.

Learn Something Useful

Learn more about those things about which you have little or no interest and you will find yourself becoming fascinated by the subject. The more you know about something, the more your enthusiasm soars. Make an effort to learn all you can about people—ask about their occupation, their families, their hobbies, their dreams and ideas. Keep asking and you're certain to find something to get enthusiastic about. The more you get to know people, the more attractive you will find them.

The Power of Visualization

Imagination powerfully influences successful outcomes. When imagination and will-power compete, the imagination always wins. Force of will never keeps you striving for success, but proper visualization will. Visualization will make you a winner on the golf course or tennis court and it will enable you to be more success-ful in business and your daily life.

All peak performers visualize success. Before shoot-ing a free throw, skilled basketball players see the ball ripping through the net. Before great golfers hit each ball, they vividly picture where they want the ball to go.

Likewise, when we visualize a pleasant and con-tented family life, we will most likely have a happy home. And visualizing business success enhances a good outcome.

A relaxed mind enforces the effectiveness of visual-ization. Practice this exercise: Assume a relaxed posi-tion. Close your eyes. Silently repeat these words, *"Breathe in relaxation; breathe out tension."* When you feel relaxed, visualize what you want to happen. Focus on this positive visual image for a few seconds. Open your eyes and hit the golf ball 250 yards straight down the middle of the fairway....or the tennis serve deep into the backhand corner....or successfully complete that sales call....or peacefully persuade your truculent child to go to his room.

Beyond Positive Thinking

A balanced life—a life filled with time's blessings—goes beyond positive thinking toward a life filled with love. An abundant life overflowing with love allows us to experience joy each day. From love comes compassion for others, discerning affection for ourselves, and the boun-tiful blessings of God.

Self-Love

Gaze affectionately into the mirror and repeat, *"You are so beautiful. You are so wonderful. I love you so."* Is that self-love? No, that's narcissism and a psychoanalyst will put you on the couch for that. Besides, you know what happened to Narcissus, don't you? The beautiful Greek youth gazed at his own refection in a pool, pined away, and was changed into the flower that bears his name. The psychological term, narcissism, describing a neurotic obsession with one's own person is derived from that story.

Healthy self love has nothing to do with narcissism. Self-love involves developing our talents while, at the same time, humbly accepting our limitations.

When we love ourselves we appreciate our uniqueness. We learn something new each day; work on improving our personality and character; allow our feelings to sparkle with goodwill; laugh often and loudly; feel the joy of daily experiences; recognize the need for affection and tenderness; and bring delight into relationships. Loving ourselves grows with our spiritual awareness of the omniscient, omnipresent God who is the source of all love.

If you have difficulty loving yourself, understand that God loves you anyway. God wants the best for you. There's nothing you can do to escape the compassionate, forgiving and accepting love of God. Studying scriptures regularly—daily—will help you understand the heart and mind of God. Comprehending God's incredible love for you will enable you to love yourself.

Loving Others

A flash of enthusiasm, the excitement of anticipation, a spark of kindness, a hearty laugh—these emotions make us more real to others—and more loving. Believing that we are loveable encourages us to step out in faith—take risks and do something for someone. When we love others we become loved in return which increases our self acceptance. Give to others and we give to ourselves. Sow love and we reap love. Altruism—what Aristotle called enlightened selfishness—provides joy that increases health and well being.

How can we become more loving? By bringing encouragement, optimism, and hope to all that we meet. By helping others feel comfortable in our presence. By spreading joy and goodwill. By being concerned about the wishes and desires of others. By understanding, caring, accepting, and forgiving. By becoming more concerned about helping others and less interested in our individual desires.

Loving others means wishing them well, just as we wish ourselves well. Here are some ways to wish others well:

- Treat others the way you would like to be treated.
- When you start to criticize others, remember that you are imperfect, too.
- Refuse to say anything bad about anyone—even if what you say is true.
- Decline to participate in gossip.
- Find something good in everyone.
- Don't complain about others.
- Praise honestly and sincerely.
- Say *"Thank you"*...a lot.
- Become genuinely interested in others.
- Smile...a lot.
- Always remember the other person's name.
- Listen more than you talk.
- Make the other person feel important, sincerely.
- Always avoid arguments.
- Avoid sarcasm or put-down humor.
- Try to see things from the other person's point of view.
- Avoid talking about other's mistakes.
- Encourage others.

Love of God

How do we love God? By appreciating all we have been given and being grateful for opportunities and challenges. We love God by loving ourselves, having faith in the power of good, doing our best to help others, and by choosing to cultivate an abundant, joy-filled life.

To increase our love for God we commune with him every day. We study the scriptures. Pray. Meditate on His love. We ask God help us build a relationship with

Him—to be in His will in all things. We worship God with others. This unending spiritual journey will continue to bless us with a love for God's unsearchable judgements, His inscrutable ways, and His tender mercies.

Summary

With each new day our happiness depends more on our attitude than our circumstances. If an abundant life ... depends on our choices—and it does—why not choose happiness now? Why not choose happiness every day? The following ten choices summarize the essence of living life positively:

1. *I choose, this day, to* be happy.

2. *I choose, this day, to* adjust myself to what comes my way.

3. *I choose, this day, to* take care of my body by exercising and eating properly.

4. *I choose, this day, to* improve my mind by reading and listening.

5. *I choose, this day, to* do something good for someone.

6. *I choose, this day, to* praise the good around me.

7. *I choose, this day, to* eliminate hurry and indecision from my life.

8. *I choose, this day, to* have a quiet half hour all by myself to think of God.

9. *I choose, this day, to* love and believe that those I love, love me.

10. *I choose, this day, to* make the choices that will bring a fulfilled life each day.

Time for Healing

Health is Wealth

A cheerful heart is good medicine,
but a crushed spirit dries up the bones.
                                    -- Proverbs 17:22

*e*motional stress is directly related to physical illness ... the more stress, the more sickness.

While we usually think of stress in terms of high
activity—meeting deadlines, fighting traffic, making
sales in a difficult market—new information shows that
the body also recognizes quieter forms of stress.
Depression decreases the immune response. Loneliness
increases mortality rates.

At the other end of the spectrum, love and joy
improve health. Cuddling doubles growth rate in infants
and children. Affection cuts cholesterol levels in half.
Those who answer affirmatively to two questions, *"Are
you happy?"* and *"Do you enjoy your job?"* have half the
risk of heart disease than those who are discontented.
Joy and happiness tend to override the other cardiac
risk factors such as high blood pressure, obesity, and
smoking.

Positive emotions—love, hope, joy, courage, confidence, enthusiasm—heal. Negative emotions—worry,
anger, depression, guilt, anxiety, grief, burnout,
distress—make us sick, emotionally and physically.

Because illness robs us of time while, conversely,
good health enables us to maximize our time, under-

standing the benefits of a healthy mind-body interaction empowers all of us live more productive lives.

The Mind-Body Connection

Research involving the mind-body connection (called psychoneuroimmunology) can be summarized in one sentence: The cerebral cortex (the thinking part of the brain) is connected to the limbic area (the feeling part of the brain) that is linked to the hypothalamus (the hormone control button of the brain) that, in turn, influences the rest of the body through a series of extremely complex microbiological connections.

When we have a thought or a feeling, our brains make chemicals known as neuropeptides. These protein-like molecules attach to the receptor sites of blood cells in the body allowing brain and body cells to talk to each other chemically. Immune cells that repair tissue, heal wounds, ingest bacteria, and protect us from cancer, have receptors for these neuropeptide chemical messengers.

Messages flowing between the brain and the immune cells are transported instantaneously. When we experience joy, the white blood cells receive that message immediately. Conversely, when we are unhappy, a negative message is transmitted directly to the white blood cells. Thus, our emotional reaction influences physical health. Positive message, good health. Negative message, poor health.

What's more intriguing, scientists have discovered certain cells in the body can make the same chemicals that the brain makes when it thinks. Our body cells make harmful or beneficial chemicals, depending on our mood. *"A cheerful heart is good medicine, but a crushed spirit dries up the bones ..."* (Proverbs 17:22) is more than a metaphor. Likewise, there may be biological truth in the statements, *"He's a pain in the neck,"* or *"She makes me sick."*

While cultivating positive emotions is healthy, getting rid of negative emotions is also beneficial to the mind and body. Because good health maximizes time, let's look at ways to eliminate negative emotions.

Managing Worry

Regretting the past or fretting about the future will always ruin a perfectly good day. Regret, a malicious worry, interferes with happiness by keeping us stuck in the past. How can we enjoy today when we are regretting the past? Worry—negative goal setting—consumes energy that could be used for productive problem solving.

The French philosopher Montaigne wrote, *"My life has been full of terrible misfortunes, most of which never happened."* Most of what we dread never occurs and our worries only interfere with our ability to solve problems.

Instead of regretting and fretting, practice emptying your mind of negative thoughts and replacing them with peaceful, tranquil ideas—thoughts that are true, noble, right, pure, lovely, admirable, and praiseworthy. If fretting continues to plaque you, write down your worries and follow this three step process:

1. What is the worst that could happen?

2. Agree to accept the worst.

3. Decide to improve upon the worst.

Then crumple up that piece of paper containing your worries and throw it in the trash. Every time a negative thought pops into your mind tell yourself, *"My worries are in the trash"* and go about the business of doing something to improve your life.

Faith in God provides the best worry solution. Read Psalms. Pray. Know that the love of God that transcends all understanding can fill your heart and mind with peace.

Handling Anger

Anger can be appropriate or inappropriate. Constructive anger, if used to strengthen relationships, can be utilized to correct a problem, right an injustice, or defend the innocent. If vented thoughtlessly, anger can destroy relationships. If suppressed, anger can cause bitterness or consume us from within. (Some psychoanalysts believe that depression is anger turned against the self.)

When someone has angered you, clearing the air and making appropriate suggestions for change will prevent deterioration in a relationship and produce needed corrections in behavior. Use the following approach to vent anger in a way that strengthens relationships:

- Meet alone—behind closed doors—with the person who has incurred your wrath.

- Tell the person what you're upset about.

- Let the person know how you feel about the problem.

- Be quiet a few seconds and let the person feel how your feel.

- Work together to formulate a solution for the difficulty.

- Tell the person what you like about his behavior.

- Shake hands.

- When it's over, it's over.

Three types of inappropriate anger impair relationships and devour our time:

- Anger over selfish demands.

- Anger from perfectionistic demands.

- Anger that results from fear of rejection or fear of harm.

How do we determine appropriateness when we are angry? Counting to ten helps. Pull back. Get away from the situation. Think. Ask yourself:

- *"Am I being selfish? Am I angry because I want more than I need."*

- *"Are my demands unreasonable? Am I expecting too much of myself and others?"*

- *"Am I afraid of being rejected or hurt?"*

An affirmative answer to any of these questions indicate that you have the problem. Continue to cool off by soothing your inappropriate emotions. Diminish selfishness by thinking of the difficulties others have. Remind yourself that no one is perfect. Be forgiving—of yourself and others. If you get angry because you feel unloved, remember that anger increases the probability of rejection. Improve your attitude about yourself and you will improve the way others respond to you.

Defeating Depression

A national survey found that the lifetime prevalence of any psychiatric disorder was 48%. Translated, this means that over the course of a lifetime one out of two people will suffer an emotional illness. *One out of two!*

The 12 month prevalence of all psychiatric disorders was close to 30%. This means that in any given time almost one of three people will demonstrate signs and symptoms of psychiatric disorder. That brings up the old joke used in speeches *"... look at the person to the left of you; look to the right; if they're OK, ... you're it."*

But psychiatric illness is no laughing matter. For the moment, let's forget about quality of life issues and look at the estimated monetary cost of one psychiatric disorder—depression—with a lifetime prevalence of 19%. The economic cost of depression in the United States has been computed to be $43.7 billion—about 75% of this cost is attributed to reduced productivity. The annual economic cost of depression is slightly higher than the annual cost of coronary artery disease which is computed at $43 billion.

Depression, a terrible disease, robs us of money, happiness, and time. Because almost three out of four people with depression never seek medical treatment, let's look at some of the early indications of depression. We'll cover just those characteristics that deal with the way depressed people think.

Depressed people:

- Possess a negative view of the past, present, and future.

- Magnify negative experiences and discount positive ones.

- Remember negative events at the expense of positive ones.

- Use *"should," "ought,"* and *"must"* a great deal when talking: *"I should study longer." "I ought to go the library more." "I must pass this test."*

- Make all or nothing statements: *"If I don't pass this test, I'll never get into medical school."*

- Demonstrate a vicious cycle of negative thinking, depressed mood, and wasted activity.

Severe depression—characterized by sleep disturbance, changes in appetite, decreased libido, feelings of hopelessness and suicidal ideation—requires medication and clinical treatment. Milder forms of depression can be handled by a change in our attitudes and actions. Here are some tips:

Think and talk positively. Instead of seeing life half-empty, pour yourself into life and, as water in a glass, fill it up. Don't waste time ruminating and criticizing. Stop blaming. Be alert to your negative thoughts and words and replace them immediately with something positive. Talk like a happy person and you'll become a happy person. Pretend you're happy and you'll be amazed at the difference this assumption will make. The power of positive thinking packs a pleasant punch.

Do your best. Give up the quest for perfection and appreciate your best effort. Know your capabilities and feel good about your attempt. Just do your best. That's all anyone can do.

Cultivate optimism. Optimism creates energy that allows you to find a way to succeed. Remember your successes; forget your failures. Visualize good things happening to you each day. Concentrate on the things you like about yourself and your life.

Rid yourself of negative talk. Expunge *"should," "ought,"* and *"must"* from your vocabulary.

Exercise. Vigorous exercise—twenty to thirty minutes of jogging, swimming, brisk walking, cycling, aerobic dance—improves circulation, increases metabolic rate, and enhances a sense of well being. Exercise increases brain neurotransmitters that help boost energy and enthusiasm. The exhaustion that depressed people experience is caused by mental fatigue, not physical fatigue. Physical exercise enhances mental alertness.

Eat right. Complex carbohydrates—fruits and vegetables—stimulate brain serotonin, a neurotransmitter that improves mood. Protein—found in chicken, fish, and lean beef—improves alertness and mental energy.

Rest. Overwork contributes to a depressed mood.

Don't take yourself too seriously. A cosmic sense of humor—the ability to laugh at yourself and your mistakes—is one of five character traits that protect against depression. (The others are anticipation—positive planning for the future; suppression—avoiding thinking about challenges until they present themselves to be solved; altruism—giving to others; and sublimation—channeling aggressive and sexual urges into productive work).

Stay active. Abraham Lincoln said, *"I must lose myself in action, lest I wither in despair."* Activity is the antidote for depression. We can remind ourselves of Churchill's axiom, *"Most of the world's work is done by people who do not feel very well."* Work cures misery.

Confront problems. When a conflict occurs, deal with the difficulty immediately. Avoiding a problem increases depression and frustration. Speak up. Don't bottle your feelings or nurse grudges.

Wear brightly colored clothes. Reds, yellows, oranges enhance mood. These are good colors for women to wear. But, men, if we wear an orange suit they will think we are manic and lock us up—which would be very depressing.

Change. Life is too short to be miserable. Be receptive to new ideas. Take risks. Step out and step up. Find a job that you enjoy. Follow your bliss.

THE HEALING POWER OF GRIEF

After a tragic loss—a loved one dies, we lose our job, we move for a home that gave us comfort—the stages of grief confront us: denial, anger, bargaining, depression, and, finally, acceptance. During the first few weeks of loss, we are numb. Everything we do takes extra effort, like walking in wet sand. Next, we begin to feel anger. We blame others or ourselves or God for the loss. The anger passes and we second guess ourselves.

We try to make deals. We search for alternatives. Then we become depressed. We feel empty. Life, for a while, loses its meaning.

Many times these stages are all wrapped into one. The feelings may descend on us all together or different feelings may come at different times. Initially, we will feel that we can never get over the loss. But, as time goes by we usually do—although, from time to time, treasured memories and special days bring, briefly, a melancholy mood. Eventually, through experiencing a wide range of moods and talking about our feelings— through tears and sorrow—acceptance comes. We read Shakespeare's *Sonnet 30* and are comforted: *"When to sessions of sweet silent thought, I summon up remembrance of things past...all losses are restored and sorrows end."*

Grieving helps us mature and grow spiritually. We incorporate the character and the spirit of the loved one, the loved place, the loved position into our own being. Because we experienced love and grieved love lost, we appreciate more life's precious moments. Grief, resolved, gives us the power to be kind and assures us that life goes on forever and ever.

Overcoming Guilt

There are two types of guilt: guilt that motivates us to change our behavior *and* guilt that punishes us just enough to allow us to keep doing those things we feel guilty about. Guilt is only helpful if it moves us toward better actions in the future.

Although many of us tend to blame ourselves for our poor judgment, guilt over past mistakes helps no one. Bad judgment does not make us bad people. The best we can do when we have made an error in judgment is to rid ourselves of guilty feelings by learning from our mistakes. Ruminating over mistakes reinforces negative mind patterns and we may repeat the very action we are trying to avoid.

We do best when we learn from our mistakes and move on. Each day speak better. Think better. Act Better. Learn. Look ahead. Make plans. Do something for someone else.

If you feel guilty about something that you know is wrong there is an easy solution—***STOP IT!*** Stop rationalizing. Stop wringing your hands. Stop feeling sorry for yourself. Stop doing what you know is wrong. Stop wasting time doing wrong things. Stop bad behavior and *start enjoying your life and your time.*

Time to Forgive

Richard Coss, once badest of the bad, meanest of the mean, is now a prison minister. An ex-con, Coss gives God praise for his changed life. A remarkable man—ebullient, articulate, empathetic, honest—he devotes his life traveling in his beat-up, two-tone rust and gray 1976 Buick offering hope to the disconsolate denizens of death row and the downtrodden deadbeats of democracy's dungeons. Down on their God, down on their country, down on their family, down on their future, the doomed make discipling difficult. But Coss, knowing the rewards of persistent compassion, keeps witnessing for better choices.

When the Alfred P. Murrah building blew up on April 19, 1995, in Oklahoma City, his two grandsons died in the blast. Coss wrote convicted bomber Timothy McVeigh that he had forgiven him: *"I love you. I forgive you. I care about you and I would pray one day that you'd accept Jesus as your savior and become a Christian."*

Reflect on the situation. Coss has loved and forgiven the man who killed his grandchildren. Could I do that? Could you?

Hate, resentment, bitterness destroy our joy by eating at our hearts and stealing our time. When we forgive—no matter how heinous the act—we free ourselves for love and life. Almost three decades ago a Yale professor wrote a mushy novel, *Love Story*, loosely based on one of his student's struggles with leukemia. The book, a huge success, became a box office smash starring Ryan O'Neil and Ali McGraw. The novel and movie is perhaps most famous for these words, *"Love means never having to say you are sorry."*

That false statement, perpetuated on a generation of gullible romantics, impairs relationships.

Harmonious relationships depend on our ability to apologize. *"I'm sorry,"* heals emotional wounds. Love means always having to say you are sorry, when you are.

All of us at one time or another have done something purposely or inadvertently that has offended someone. When we are wrong, let's admit it quickly and emphatically. If we wish to be forgiven, we must first forgive those who have offended us. We would live pleasantly if we could forgive each other (and ourselves). Love—unconditional positive concern—means leaving our grudges behind and ignoring the flaws in others.

The search for forgiveness is universal. Ernest Hemingway's short story, *The Capital of the World,* told of a Spanish father and his son, Paco, whose strained relationship reached a breaking point. Paco ran away from home. The father, after traveling around Spain in search of his rebellious son, put an add in the Madrid newspaper that read, *"Dear Paco, meet me in front of the Madrid newspaper office tomorrow at noon. All is forgiven. I love you."* The next morning 800 *"Pacos"* gathered at the church, all seeking forgiveness. Paco is a very common name in Spain. So is the desire for forgiveness, the world over.

Mastering Anxiety

One out of four people will have some sort of anxiety disorder sometime during their lifetime. The annual cost of anxiety disorders in the United States is approximately $46.6 billion. 75% of this monetary loss is due to decreased work productivity and an inefficient use of time.

Some anxiety disorders—severe generalized anxiety, panic attacks, compulsions, and post traumatic stress—require medical treatment. Milder conditions respond to relaxation techniques and changing the way we think about challenges.

A simple relaxation technique has proved useful in diminishing the vicious cycle of worry and muscle tension. The more we worry the tighter our muscles get, the more tense we become the more we worry. Follow this technique to relax:

• Sit in a comfortable position.

- Close your eyes.
- Breathe in deeply and as you do so visualize breathing in relaxation.
- When you breathe out, visualize breathing out tension.
- The deep breathing will, by itself, help your muscles relax.
- Next, silently repeat a phrase or word over and again. Any word will do: *"Love." "Joy." "Peace." "_____."*

During this relaxation period you may choose to repeat a favorite Bible passage or meditate on God's love and peace. Remain in this relaxed state of mind and body for twenty to thirty minutes. Research has show that practicing this healing silence two times daily has numerous benefits including:

- Decrease in heart rate, blood pressure, and muscle tension.
- Decrease in the stress hormones ACTH and cortisone.
- Decreased muscle tension, irritability, and subjective anxiety.
- Decreased tobacco and alcohol use.
- Increased self-confidence, mental clarity, vitality, and creativity.

After mastering the healing silence you can practice a ten second relaxation exercise throughout the day to prevent the build-up of tension. During the ten second exercise breathe in deeply, repeating silently to yourself, *"Breathe in relaxation."* Hold your breath and visualize a peaceful scene. Then breathe out silently repeating, *"Breathe out tension."* This ten second exercise repeated as often as necessary throughout the day will restore your energy while relieving your tension.

Overcoming the Overworked Trap

The overwork trap weaves its tangled web insidiously. We have so much to do we can't seem to get it all done.

We get busier and busier and we fail to catch up.

The harder we work, the more mistakes we make.

The more mistakes we make, the harder we work.

Because of the mistakes we make, the further behind we get.

This frenetic activity can escalate to produce symptoms of burnout or overwork:

- Multiple physical complaints:
    headaches
    backaches
    stomachaches

- Restless sleep and fatigue.

- Emotional disturbance:
    apathy
    worry
    irritability
    depression
    anxiety

- Dreading going to work, reduced work performance and/or impaired productivity.

- Joyless striving and resistance to change.

- Impaired relationships with friends, family, and associates.

- A growing sense of disliking the client or customer.

Preventing burnout comes from recognizing our limitations and seeking variety and balance in our lives. We may be unable to change our environmental stresses, but we can adapt a more moderate response to those stresses by doing the best we can and learning to protect our time.

Duke University psychiatrist, John Rhoads, MD, studied successful, effective, and healthy executives who worked at least sixty hours weekly and compared these individuals with executives who developed burnout from working over sixty hours weekly.

Look at the difference between the *"winners"* and *"losers."*

Winners	*Losers*
Solve problems	Ruminate about problems
Rest when tired	When fatigued, work longer hours
Avoid drug and alcohol abuse	Use drugs and alcohol as an escape
Enjoy scheduled vacations	Postpone vacations
Have a supportive family life	Have a chaotic family life
Cultivate friendships	Avoid friendships
Engage in regular exercise	Have a sedentary life style
Display varied interests	Have few interests
Enjoy a sense of humor	Unable to laugh at self

To prevent overwork we would do well to follow these common sense rules for living a balanced life:

Rest before you get tired. Recognize signs of fatigue before you get frustrated. Take an afternoon or a long weekend away from work. When you return you'll be amazed how much more you get accomplished. A Carnegie Institute study confirms the importance of regular rest. Men loading pig iron who rested for 34 seconds after working for 26 seconds were able to load 40 tons in an 8 hour shift. Normal crews who never rested loaded only 12 tons.

Alternate activities. Energy can be acquired by splitting up the day into the smallest possible segments of time. Break your work into small compartments, get something accomplished and then go on to the next small compartment.

Exercise. Most of us run out of energy because of mental fatigue. Physical exercise gets the overwork webs out of our brains and invigorates our thoughts.

Reward yourself. To create energy, reward yourself every time you accomplish a task. Pat yourself on the back, take a short breather, go have some fun, give yourself a spell of pleasurable laziness.

Build leisure into your lifestyle. Take regularly scheduled vacations. Plan a half day off occasionally. Rest is an excellent use of time and properly scheduled recreation will increase productivity.

Combat boredom. Boredom, the greatest energy drain, can be defeated by having variety in your life and work. Setting daily, weekly, and monthly goals can make work fun and help you feel satisfied when a task is accomplished.

Laugh and enjoy yourself. Ask yourself, *"Am I having fun yet?"* If not, why not? Figure a way to bring fun to the workplace.

Take time for family and friends. Here's what Lee Iacocca, former CEO of Chrysler Corporation said: *"Since college I've worked hard during the week and, except for crises, kept my weekends free for family and recreation...I'm amazed at the number of people who can't seem to control their own schedules. 'Boy,' some say, 'I worked so hard last year I didn't even take a vacation.' I say, 'You dummy. You mean to tell me you can take the responsibility of an 80 million dollar project and you can't take two weeks out of the year to have some fun?'"*

Summary

Life is difficult.

Tragedy happens.

People disappoint.

We can't change life's challenges. We can't change other people and events.

But we can change our thoughts and beliefs about life's misfortunes and consequently have healthy, productive lives.

Peace, happiness, joy, and fulfillment come from within.

Time for Freedom

A Chance To Be Better

Ill habits gather by unseen degrees –
As brooks make rivers, rivers run to seas.
                                        -- Ovid

*M*any of us, at one time or another, find our-selves victims of our own bad habits.

These habits may seem harmless initially, but grad-ually and progressively, they begin to dominate our lives. A passing pleasure turns into a persistent prob-lem. We become slaves to our habits. Let's take a look at the most common life imprisoners—and how to free our-selves from their chains.

Preventing Alcohol Abuse

Alcoholism is the number one health problem in the United States.

♦ Of the estimated 100 million Americans who con-sume alcoholic beverages, one out of ten (approximately 9-10 million) becomes a problem drinker.

♦ Almost 20% of all hospital care expenses result from alcohol abuse.

♦ Untreated alcoholism decreases life expectancy by ten to twelve years and leads to an increased inci-dence of liver and heart disease.

♦ Alcohol is implicated in 50% of traffic accidents, 50% of homicides, 30% of rapes, 80% of robberies, 33% of suicides, and 62% of child abuse cases.

✦ The cost of alcoholism is astronomical; the loss of time secondary to alcohol abuse, unfathomable; and the impairment to a balanced life, immeasurable.

Alcoholics have an uncanny ability to cover up their problems, but eventually alcohol abuse leads to conflicts with family or friends, legal problems, and job difficulties. Are you an alcoholic? Take this quiz:

O   Have you consumed alcohol daily for one month or more?

O   Do you get into difficulty with family or friends because of your drinking?

O   Has alcohol caused you to get into legal difficulties?

O   Do you get into frequent fights or arguments while drinking?

O   Do you have a compelling desire to use alcohol?

O   Have you gone on drinking binges lasting for two or more days?

O   Have you felt the need to cut down on your drinking?

O   Have you ever felt annoyed by criticism of your drinking?

O   Have you ever had guilty feelings about your drinking?

O   Do you ever take a morning eye-opener?

An affirmative answer to any of the questions suggests a problem with alcohol. The more *"yes"* responses the bigger the problem. Remember: If you are an alcoholic, because your drinking problem includes denial of the disease, you will be the last person to realize you have an illness, and you will want to discount the significance of affirmative answers on this simple quiz. Eliminating denial is always the first step to freedom from alcohol.

By far the best treatment for alcohol abuse is the hard and narrow path of total abstinence. Abstinence can best be achieved through regularly attending Alcoholics Anonymous meetings.

It's much easier, of course, to prevent alcohol abuse than to treat the problem. In preventing alcohol abuse, you must remember that alcoholism is insidious—it can creep up on you. You may drink to relax at the end of a stressful day, combat loneliness, reduce inhibitions, make yourself feel powerful, or to take the edge off problems at work or home. The following recommendations will help modify your drinking habits and prevent the insidious development of alcoholism:

Don't take a drink every time one is offered.

Try non-alcoholic drinks for cocktails: Perrier or tonic water with a twist of lime, club soda and orange juice, etc.

Drink only for enjoyment, not because of boredom, depression, frustration, anxiety, or worry.

Instead of guzzling drinks, sip alcoholic beverages slowly.

Set limits on the time you drink. You may want to eliminate week-day drinking and avoid business lunch drinking. How about not drinking before 5:00 pm?

Limit the number of drinks you have each day. Cut down slowly if you are a moderate to heavy drinker. Eliminate one drink a day each week until you're down to no more than two drinks daily.

Resolve never to get intoxicated.

Use exercise as a stress reliever instead of alcohol.

Meditation, contemplative prayer, or the relaxation response can reduce the craving for alcohol.

Combating Drug Abuse

For some, drugs seem to be a way to deal with disappointment and add zest to a boring lifestyle.

Unfortunately, drugs, while often making us feel better at the time of use, always produce depressed feelings after the drug is withdrawn. Hence, there is a tendency to return to the drug over and again to get relief from emotional distress. The antidote? Prevention. Here are some suggestions to guard against drug abuse:

- Never use recreational drugs!
- The abuse of minor tranquilizers can be insidious. Avoid them.
- Watch your use of analgesics containing narcotics.
- There is hardly ever any need for a sleeping pill, except for brief periods of time during severe stress, or when defeating *"jet lag."*

Stop the Tobacco Habit, Now!

Smoking one pack of cigarettes a day shortens life by eight to nine years and significantly increases the risk of cancer, heart disease, stroke and upper respiratory infections.

Nicotine addiction makes giving up the tobacco habit difficult. The first few weeks you stop smoking, you'll be irritable, anxious, perspire, have abdominal cramps, muscle spasms, and increased appetite.

The psychological aspects of smoking are also unpleasant to overcome. It's a struggle to give up that urge to smoke after meals, at parties, or when you're bored or frustrated.

Here are some suggestions that will make quitting easier:

♦ Make a list of cigarette dislikes. On an index card list what you abhor about the smoking habit. Most smokers will list things like:

Health risk: I worry about cancer and heart disease.

Personal hygiene: I don't like having tobacco breath.

Expense: Cigarettes cost $850 a month.

Inconvenience: I feel like a social outcast at airports and restaurants.

Loss of control: I don't like being a slave to a cigarette.

♦ Make a list of the benefits of giving up the noxious weed. On the flip side of the index card you can list contentment gained from breaking the habit:

I'll be able to walk upstairs without panting.

I'll be able to smell and taste again.

People will stop frowning at me.

I'll be a good example for my children.

I'll feel great about my will power.

♦ Keep the card in your pocket or purse. Read your list two or three times daily.

♦ Commit to your conviction. Make certain you really want to stop smoking before you attempt to give up tobacco.

Decide to quit a week before you stop and put it in writing.

Verbalize your commitment.

Tell a close friend or relative that you are stopping cigarettes forever.

Throw away your cigarettes, your matches, and your lighters.

Discard your ashtrays.

♦ Approach stopping intelligently. Know the times that your will power is weakest so you can formulate a strategy for strengthening your resolve during your vulnerable periods. Ask associates how they stopped smoking. Perhaps their methods will help you also. Books, tapes, and organized programs are available to assist you. You may benefit from hypnosis, acupuncture, or medication. Use whatever will work for you.

♦ Be prepared. Understand that you will experience withdrawal symptoms the first few weeks after you quit. Each day remind yourself that you are one day closer to getting through withdrawal.

✦ Plan ahead. Don't let crisis situations erode your resolve. When you are tempted to light up, read your commitment aloud. Call a friend for help. Take a shower. Go for a long walk.

✦ Reward yourself. Set a series of milestones and reward yourself when you reach them.

> *Spend the money you saved from giving up smoking on something that you enjoy.*

> *Splurge! Get involved in some new activities-music lessons, a new sport, a craft.*

✦ Practice relaxation techniques. While relaxed, visualize how good you feel and how healthy you appear cigarette-free:

> *Your sense of smell and taste are sharpened.*

> *Your coughing has vanished.*

> *You have energy.*

> *You look younger and more vigorous.*

> *Your skin radiates.*

> *You have fantastic will power.*

Improve Your Sleep Time

Improving sleep patterns will save you time and increase your productivity. Because many medical conditions can cause sleep disturbance a physical examination and, perhaps, an evaluation at a sleep laboratory may be indicated if you have chronic insomnia or hypersomnia.

The most common cause of non-medical insomnia is conditioned sleep disturbance. You might have developed difficulty falling asleep because of a temporary stressful situation and learn to associate the simple process of going to bed and turning off the light with frustration and sleeplessness.

Sedatives may help temporarily, but eventually they will cause serious difficulties. Tolerance for the sedative will develop and higher doses of the medication will be required.

Stay away from sedatives. Try this prescription instead:

- **Divert your attention** *from your business activity an hour before going to bed by reading a book, preferably one on developing your people skills or a book to inspire you to reach your potential.*
  The last thing we see, hear, or read before falling to sleep tends to penetrate our unconscious better than experiences earlier in the day.

- **Go to bed** *when you feel sleepy.*
  If you fail to go to sleep in 5-10 minutes, get out of bed and return to your book.

- **Set your alarm clock** *for 6 am the next day.*
  No matter how sleepy or tired you are, get up at this time.

- **Avoid day time naps.**

- **Don't watch television in bed.**
  Watching television tends to keep you awake and remember what happens to your brain when you hear and see negative words and pictures right before falling asleep.

Summary

Those who keep themselves free from drugs and alcohol have found something better than instant gratification.

They have become vibrant, fully functioning people by replacing bad habits with a life of freedom—a life of wellness.

Freedom defenders have learned how to:

- Live in the present by focusing of future benefits.

- Promote spontaneity by allowing the expression of feelings.

- Take responsibility for behavior by expunging excuses from exclamations. (That's an alliteration for: *"They don't blame others for their problems."*)

- Continue learning by reading and attending seminars.

- Grow more loving by focusing on others.

- Develop a sense of humor by laughing at life's absurdities.

- Acquire a high energy level by finding something to get excited about.

- Defeat fatigue by taking time to rest and relax.

- Sustain physical fitness by exercising regularly and vigorously.

- Cultivate contentment by accepting imperfections and appreciating talents.

- Tolerate unexpected setbacks by understanding the Law of Mud: "... *throw enough of it on the wall and some will stick;"*

  ... or the Law of Pigs: "... *even a blind one who keeps rooting can find an acorn;"*

  ... or the Law of Ruth: "... *keep swinging hard and you'll eventually hit one out of the park."*

Those who have cultivated a life of wellness free from drugs and alcohol vibrate with energy and radiate physical fitness. When they walk into a room, light brightens and energy pulsates.

Freedom supporters offer encouragement to all they encounter. They laugh loudly, love deeply, and hope always.

Time for Fitness

Adding Years to Your Life and Life to Your Years

Do you not know that your
body is a temple of the Holy Spirit ....
-- I Corinthians 6:19

*t*aking care of your body through regular exercise and a sensible diet can become a positive habit.

The pleasure gained from maintaining a moderate exercise program and consistent, healthy eating habits will generate a fitness addiction. After you have exercised regularly and eaten properly for about twelve months, you will feel so much better physically and emotionally that you will want to continue this healthy program for your lifetime. The key to developing a positive fitness habit resides in making certain that your workouts and eating patterns bring you more pleasure than pain. The often repeated statement, *"No pain, no gain"* can be changed to, *"No pleasure, no lifetime fitness treasure."*

A Lifestyle Paradox

Our attitude toward physical health reflects a lifestyle paradox. Choose any book best seller list and you'll find at least one cookbook and one diet book. As you flip through the pages of any woman's magazine you will find articles describing how to stay trim alternating with enticing food ads. Surfing the television channels reveals food and beer commercials alternating with fitness equipment advertising. No wonder we're ambivalent about food, diet, and exercise.

Statistics mirror that ambivalence.

- Approximately 40 million Americans are at least 20% overweight.
- An additional 80 million are 10 to 15 pounds overweight.
- Half of all college females have symptoms of bulimia.
- Anorexia has reached epidemic proportions.

Fitness Failures

Many of us fail in a fitness program because we try to do too much too soon. What happens to most of us January 1st of every year? We resolve to go on a diet and exercise regularly. But the diet we choose is too restrictive—celery and carrots—so after a few days we quit in disgust. Or if we maintain that diet for more than three weeks, we turn into a rabbit and disappear down a hole.

The same sort of thing happens with our New Year Resolution Exercise Program. We pay $500 to join an exotic health spa. The first day we workout for three hours—weight training, aerobic dance, a half-mile swim in the pool, a mile jog. We get dizzy and nauseated and our muscles ache for a month and we never go back to the club.

Of course, I'm exaggerating to make a point: We tend to try to become physically fit too quickly. The physical and emotional pain we inflict upon ourselves causes us to quit before we have developed a healthy fitness habit.

Commit To Be Fit

To keep from frustrating yourself don't begin a lifestyle change until you're certain you want to do what it takes. Before beginning an exercise and fitness program ask yourself these questions:

"Do I really want to change?"

"Why do I want to change? "

"How much do I want to change?"

"What am I willing to give up to effect this change?"

"What benefits will I enjoy if I change?"

"How will my life be different if I make this change?"

"What do I need to do to assure lifelong success in maintaining this change?"

Finding the motives and benefits for lifestyle changes will allow you to commit to be fit.

Dieting: The Losing Game

Fad diets fail. Or, fad diets feed flourishing fat filled folks. Why? Going on a restrictive diet decreases your metabolic rate.

An impeded metabolic rate means you burn fat at a slower rate. The fewer calories you eat, the less energy your body burns. When you starve yourself—that's what most people do when they *"diet"*—your body releases hormones that causes you to store fat. When you return to a normal eating pattern fat continues to accumulate. The more you diet, the fatter you get.

Dieting produces a yo-yo effect with rapid weight loss (mostly water and protein) followed by weight gain (mostly fat). Dieting becomes a losing game-you get fatter and fatter with each dieting episode.

Most diets are based on two assumptions:

1. The weight you lose when dieting is mostly fat.
2. Diets do not affect the metabolic rate.

And both assumptions are false.

When you begin dieting the body uses the simplest form of available energy. This energy source is glycogen (a carbohydrate) stored in the muscles and liver. It is not fat. After providing energy by burning glycogen and shedding water, the dieter's body tends to lose both fat and muscle. Most people can't continue to eat sparingly.

Eventually they eat as much, if not more, than they ate before dieting. They rather quickly regain the weight they lost and because dieting has changed the metabolic rate most of the weight gain is fat, not muscle.

Moderation: The Only Way

Losing weight gradually, while exercising moderately, provides the only proven method for losing weight and becoming physically fit. A pound of fat contains 3500 calories. To prevent drastic changes in the metabolic rate it's best to burn those 3500 calories through a combination of diet and exercise.

To maintain a steady metabolic rate, no more than 500 extra calories should be lost each day. Burning 500 excess calories daily results in a loss of one pound of fat weekly (500 x 7 = 3500 calories). You can lose 52 pounds of fat a year using this method. And, assuming you continue a lifestyle of moderation, you will keep the weight off. You will be slim, trim, and muscular.

Some nutritionists allow grossly obese individuals to lose two pounds a week. This fast weight loss plan calls for an expenditure of 1000 excess calories daily. For those grossly overweight, several years may be required to maintain an ideal body weight even with this fast track plan. If you are after fitness and maintenance of an ideal body weight, never lose more than two pounds weekly.

A healthy, moderate diet can be maintained using the following guidelines:

> *Eat a balanced diet* consisting of 15% fat, 25% protein, and 60% complex carbohydrates—fruits, vegetables, and whole grain products.

> *Eat high fiber foods* that decrease absorption of calories by increasing transit time through the gastrointestinal system.

> *Substitute* low-calorie food for high-calorie food.

Substitute skim milk for whole milk and yogurt for ice cream.

Eat smaller portions of food. Leave a little something on your plate. Never take second helpings.

Cut down on snacks. Most people eat 500 calories in snacks daily.

Avoid salt, sugar, candy, white bread, junk food, colas, and other foods with nutritionless calories.

Drink at least eight glasses of water daily. Each glass should contain at least eight ounces of water. Water helps flush excess waste products produced when the body burns fat. Water also slightly deadens hunger pains.

Limit alcohol to 1-2 drinks daily.

Make your dinner meal the lightest of the day because your metabolic rate is lowest at night.

Instead of using the word *"diet,"* use the phrase *"changing lifestyle."*

Diet conjures unhealthy feelings such as frustration and failure. Lifestyle augers moderation.

Don't count calories. Eat sensibly and exercise moderately and you'll replace overeating with a healthier, more enjoyable way of living.

Exercise: The Energy Enhancer

Regular exercise maintains good health by helping maintain an ideal body weight, reducing mental fatigue, and relieving emotional stress.

Physical activity also improves the body's resistance to disease by stimulating the immune response.

Exercise enhances self-esteem, deepens sleep, and improves sexual vitality.

Exercise causes weight loss in two ways:

1. Exercise sustained at least twenty minutes at 75% of maximum heart rate speeds the metabolic rate during exercise.

2. The metabolic rate remains elevated for several hours following exercise and calories continue to burn at a faster than normal rate.

These pointers will help you maintain a reasonable exercise program:

Don't expect too much too soon. It may take three months before you can swim more than a few laps or walk half a mile.

Get in the habit of exercise and your fitness will gradually improve. If you're in poor shape begin exercising by walking one block daily for one week. Each week increase your walk one block.

Starting slowly will help you develop an exercise habit before physical discomfort discourages you. There is no need to suffer to get a good workout.

Work out with others. Slacking off becomes easy when you workout alone. Walking or jogging regularly with friends, joining a health club, participating in an aerobics dance class or joining a swim team are just a few ways you can build friendships while maintaining fitness.

Set weekly goals. Setting weekly fitness goals can stimulate maintenance of your fitness program. Keeping a log book of your progress can encourage you.

Don't use fatigue as an excuse. The grind of your daily routine may produce mental fatigue. The best antidote? Exercise. On the other hand, don't overdo physical activity. Muscle soreness, injuries, prolonged rapid pulse, and nausea may indicate you are trying to do too much too soon.

Have variety in your exercise program. Counter boredom by varying your activities. You can also listen to the radio, tapes, or disks while you run and you can read or watch television while on a stationary bike or stair-step machine.

Train, Don't Strain

A moderate exercise program should consist of a balance between cardiovascular conditioning, flexibility exercises, and muscle toning.

For cardiovascular conditioning walk, run, swim, or bicycle for 20-30 minutes three times weekly. Your pace is about right when you have difficulty talking when you are exercising. If you can talk easily, you would do well to speed up some. If you are gasping for air, you're exercising too vigorously.

Your heart rate can also help evaluate your exercise pace. Calculate your maximum heart rate by subtracting your age from 220. If you are 40 years old, your maximum heart rate would be 180. [220 - 40 = 180]. At the end of your exercise period you have had an excellent workout if your heart rate equals 60-80% of your maximum heart rate.

If you are 40 years old, your heart rate should range between 108 and 144. [180 x 60% = 108; 180 x 80% = 144].

Perform flexibility exercises five minutes before and after exercising. Stretch the back muscles, hamstrings, quadriceps, and Achilles tendons. To increase circulation in the extremities, walk briskly for five minutes before beginning vigorous exercise. At the completion of your workout, cool down with a five minute walk and a few more stretching exercises.

Muscle toning can begin with pushups and modified sit-ups. If you like you can add a workout with free weights or machine weights. Pushups and sit-ups when done correctly are adequate for maintaining muscle tone.

Vitamin Supplementation

In these days of processed foods, fast foods and overcooked foods, the typical modern American diet fails to provide the vitamins and minerals required to maintain excellent health.

As our bodies produce energy by using oxygen to burn carbohydrates, highly reactive chemicals called free radicals are released into our system. Tobacco smoke, vehicle exhaust, pollutants, alcohol, and emotional stress also increase the body's production of free radicals.

These free radicals cause an increased risk of cancer and heart disease by altering the structure of fat, protein, carbohydrates, and DNA molecules. Antioxidants, found in vitamins–especially beta carotene, vitamin C and vitamin E–destroy free radicals and, therefore, help prevent cancer.

Because wholesome foods contain more beneficial attributes than a few isolated vitamins and minerals, concentrates of whole plant materials are the best source for vitamin supplementation. Organic vitamins— vitamins from plants—provide phytochemicals that prevent damage from free radicals and regulate enzyme activity.

To maintain proper blood levels take water soluble vitamins (B & C), three times daily. The fat soluble vitamins can be taken once or twice daily. To provide complete benefits, vitamins should come from plant sources. The following schedule would provide adequate supplementation for a healthy adult:

- At least one multiple vitamin and mineral supplement daily.
- 15 mg. of beta carotene once daily.
- At least 250 mg. of vitamin C three times daily.
- Vitamin B complex three times daily.
- Parselenium-E (Vitamin E + the antioxidant mineral, selenium) 400 I.U./ 10 mcg. once daily.

The increased popularity of specialty supplements demand a brief listing of the most common herbs on the market today:

- Ginseng—enhances work endurance.
- Ginkgo biloba—improves blood flow to the brain.
- Coenzyme Q10 complex—improves muscle metabolism at the cellular level.

- Chromium picolinate—supports proper metabolism of fats, carbohydrates and proteins and complements weight loss programs.

- Echinacea—helps support the immune response. Use sparingly because chronic use may impair the immune response.

- Passion flower with chamomile—the "chill out" herb is excellent for tension reduction and mild sedation.

- DHEA (dehydroepiandrosterone)–a natural body steroid that decreases with aging; in its synthetic form, DHEA may increase fat burning, muscle mass and sex drive.

- St. John's Wort (or hypericum)–moreso in Europe than the U.S., this herb has been successfully used in treating mild to moderate depression.

Summary

You don't have to attain an exceptionally high level of fitness to enjoy a life of wellness.

Maintain a sensible diet and persist with a well balanced, moderate exercise program and you will add years to your life and life to your years.

And remember: all vitamin supplements, herbs and other *"over-the-counter"* medications bear certain degrees of risk and/or controversy; some *otc* products have been known to produce side-effects when taken with other medication(s); *therefore, none of these products should ever be taken without first consulting your physician.*

Time for Romance

A Radiant Blessing

Love does not consist in gazing at each other
but in looking together in the same direction.
-- Antoine de Saint Exupery

*t*he great mass of marriages fluctuate,

... between good times and bad; challenges and rewards; happiness and sadness; perplexity and indifference.

If, through the years, the husband and wife can rely on a solid foundation that can withstand the difficult times, the marriage will become a radiant blessing.

Here, then, are some ideas on the fundamentals of a stable marriage.

Commitment and Praise

Commitment to the marriage is the most important trait that parents can pass along to their children and is the basic quality that women seek in men.

Women desire self-assured men who will supply them the essential material comforts and emotional commitment. In contrast to bravado or dominance, men who have the courage to commit themselves to marriage reflect quiet confidence and self-assurance—an inner power devoid of the desire to control.

Paradoxically, because there is no desire to dominate, men with self-assurance have a magnetic quality that pulls women to them.

Men—even confident, self-assured men—want praise. They will do just about anything to get compliments from the woman they love. Men are just little boys, grown older. They require lots of approval. The number one rule for women who want a stable marriage is this: *Catch your man doing something right and praise him for it.*

And, of course, don't nag. Nagging reinforces bad behavior. Ignore bad behavior and it will diminish. Praise good behavior and it will increase.

Instead of nagging, bite your tongue until it bleeds. Wait until you find your man doing something right and then tell him, *"I'm proud of you."* Watch him beam with pleasure and enjoy the improvement in his commitment to you.

Communication

Research studies indicate that women may be more romantic and more verbal because of brain physiology. Neuroscientist have discovered that the corpus callosum–the fibers that connect the right and left hemispheres of the brain–are more prominent in women than in men, giving women more artistic and verbal skills, while men have more white matter in the brain–material that facilitates sensory and motor coordination.

Thus, men sail boats while women write poems about sailing. Women talk more; men are more active.

Please remember that I am discussing averages here. For example, most men will be taller than most women, but any one woman may be taller than any one man.

One of the most frequent complaints women have about men is *"He won't talk to me."* Husbands and wives would do well to set aside a few minutes each day to simply talk with each other. Establish some time together each day for a stroll around the neighborhood, having dinner without the television blaring, sipping coffee in bed each morning—all these possibilities can enhance communication.

Romance

Genuine love is an extension of the self. When we love, we focus on helping those we love grow emotionally, intellectually, and spiritually. We can forget our own egos by creating happiness for our loved ones. Paradoxically, the more we give of ourselves, the more we extend ourselves—the more we receive, the more we are replenished.

Enduring love, then, is an act of will. Enduring love transcends emotion.

Keeping Romance Alive

The key to keeping romance alive is regular dating and courting. It's important to set aside one night a week to go out together. Dining at a gourmet restaurant (or even a fast food restaurant as long as you take time to be together without the children) or a night of dancing or an evening at the movies can help keep the romance alive.

To maintain the sparkle in a marriage, husband and wife would do well to schedule a weekend away from home once a month. This monthly excursion adds an anticipatory excitement to the marriage. Scheduling this engagement on the calendar and sticking with the plan to get away, no matter what, will reinforce commitment to the relationship.

Have variety on these weekend excursions. Alternate a trip to the city with a visit to a guest ranch or a lake resort. Perhaps a weekend camping trip would be just the twist required to keep the marriage stimulating and fresh. Regular trips away from children, friends, and the hassles of work engender a successful marriage.

If finances seem to challenge a week-end trip, remember it's getting away that is important, not the distance from home or the amount of money spent. For example, if you live in San Antonio a short trip to Austin would be fairly inexpensive. Or if you live in Austin you can drive to San Antonio. If you live in Poteet, you can go anywhere and have a romantic time.

Children and career plans can interfere with the spark of marriage unless a concerted effort is made to keep the honeymoon freshness alive. Annual trips together without family and friends can enrich the marriage. Have variety in these annual "honeymoons"—a ski resort one year, a Caribbean cruise the next, a trip to Europe the third. You may have to spend the fourth year in a pup tent at a state park. *Only a lack of imagination-and money-can limit the vacation possibilities.*

Women appreciate being romanced. They enjoy a walk on the beach holding hands. They like sitting out on the patio when the moon is full. They enjoy having their birthdays, anniversaries, and Valentine's Day remembered. They get excited about spontaneous gifts.

Remember: *A rose in time is more valuable than a one thousand dollar gift too late. It's also less expensive.*

Men, on a routine day send your wife a flower with this note: *"To an extraordinary woman on an ordinary day."* That's romantic. You'll make her happy and consequently you'll be happier.

A life of moderation and regular exercise can also keep the marriage spark burning. The key to exercise is consistency—keeping after it year after year. Joining a health club or spa that offers a wide range of exercise opportunities—aerobics, handball, racquetball, Nautilus and free weight workouts, calisthenics, saunas, Jacuzzi—can add variety that encourages a lifelong habit of romance-enhancing physical fitness.

Intimacy

There appear to be some gender differences between male and female sexual arousal. Hugs, caresses, and gentle kissing are more arousing to women's sensuality than visual stimuli. In contrast, visual stimuli are generally more exciting for men.

Not only do women need more hugs and shows of affection on a day-to-day basis, they also need more caressing and more foreplay to fully enjoy the sexual act.

Unfortunately, some men have a difficult time demonstrating physical affection. Men, if you have this problem, work on improving your ability to feel comfortable with the physical demonstrations of affection. Just practice hugging or kissing her every day. And it's all right to just hold your lover without it leading to anything else.

As with other types of communication, men and women, in general, have different ways of achieving sexual arousal. For men, parise and appreciation is prized, while women seek security, meaningful conversation, romance, and hugs and kisses prior to sexual intimacy.

Open communication enhances sexual intimacy. When men and women talk with each other about desires, sex becomes fun, adventurous, and stimulating. And being honest about feelings builds trust and closeness.

Summary

Commitment, communication, romance, and intimacy uphold a solid relationship. Attention to these fundamentals keep marriage on a solid foundation.

Enduring love—commitment to continuing concern—requires *giving a little, taking a little,*

... laughing a little, crying a little,

... winning a little, losing a little,

... letting our poor hearts break a little.

As lovers we're receptive, understanding, forgiving, and engaged in the present moment. Throughout the days, words of love whispered soft and true, provide passion for living an abundant life.

Love, more lovely and temperate than a summer's day, brings delight to share with those who care. Forever delivering warmth to marriage, the ultimate romance, renders the replenishing gift, the radiant blessing of love.

Time for Family

The Warm Hearth of Home

Where shall a man find sweetness to surpass his own home and parents?
In far lands he shall not, though he find a house of gold.
-- Homer's Odyssey

*b*eing a parent is a perplexing privilege.

Parents must be relaxed and forgiving while at the same time being immovable when the situation calls for firmness. This dichotomy of purpose is what makes parenting so difficult. It's an uneasy balance between rules and freedom, passion and prudence.

Parenthood requires flexibility. Observant parents realize that every child has a different personality, a distinct set of coping mechanisms. Parents who learn nuances of behavior can maximize each child's potential. And, most important, parents who cultivate patience and a sense of humor can enjoy their children.

In this chapter, we'll discuss ways that parents can walk that thin and narrow tightrope of parenthood—how they can maintain their parental balance that allows them time to treasure moments with their children.

Secure Parents Make Good Parents

Becoming a good parent by following rules and regulations is similar to learning brain surgery through correspondence. Good surgeons master the fundamentals. So must parents.

To be a good parent requires that we cultivate a reliable foundation of core values—integrity, faith, and self-discipline. We first must be confident and hopeful. Secure parents make good parents.

Security comes from knowing our words and actions are true to our convictions. Secure parents have correct priorities: God first; family second; career third.

Good parents study God's word. They must fully agree with God's plan, pledge themselves to obey it, and put His principles into action:

> *Faithfully obey the commands I am giving you today—to love the Lord your God and to serve him with all your heart and with all your soul...Fix these words of mine in your hearts and minds; tie them as symbols on your hands and bind them on your foreheads. Teach them to your children, talking about them when you sit at home and when you walk along the road, when you lie down and when you get up.*
> -- Deuteronomy 11:13,18-19

Love and Respect

Love, real love, means accepting our children exactly as they are, while encouraging them to grow emotionally, intellectually and spiritually. Love means we demand less and encourage more. A loving parent is also not hesitant to show tenderness—to give hugs, kisses and pats on the back.

Love, of course, is more than affection. Love requires setting aside time for children. When children are small, we can hold them on our laps and read to them. Reading with children when they're very young, a wonderful way to spend rich time with them, combines learning, imagination and touch.

As children mature we can go on walks with them, camp, and fish together. Attending a child's school functions, music concerts, tennis matches, and reward ceremonies builds self-esteem, and gives the entire family memories to treasure.

If we want children to act maturely, we must treat them with respect. As parents we learn to master the difficult task of allowing our children freedom to make mistakes while providing guidance to prevent the mistakes from being big ones.

Being a parent is like handling an eaglet—you've got to hold on tightly to keep it from flying away prematurely, yet hold gently enough so it won't be squeezed to death.

Respect requires catching our children doing something right and anticipating good behavior from them. Children tend to perform the way we expect them to perform. When we verbalize positive expectations good things happen.

Teaching Responsible Behavior

Parents must model the character traits they want their children to possess. If we want self-reliant children we must be reliable ourselves. We must keep our promises to ourselves and others. Our actions must speak so loudly that others cannot hear what we are saying. Deeds are much better instructors than words. Here are some guidelines for firm, consistent parenting:

Avoid Over-gratification

The first three years of life, children need attention, comfort and protection. But constant attention can be just as damaging as giving them unlimited amounts of candy and sweets. Over-gratification produces an infantile, self-centered adult.

To cure children from attention addiction, put your marriage first. A healthy marriage provides a secure foundation on which children can build self-esteem, autonomy and independence.

Don't be a slave to your children. If you are making three or four trips a day hauling them from place to place you are traveling too much. Decide on the important functions and set limits.

Take Charge

Parents must have the courage of their convictions. *Don't bargain. Don't plead. Don't bribe. Don't threaten. Don't give second chances.* You cannot win when you try to reason with children

Eloquent explanations mean nothing. When a parent makes a decision and the child screams *"Why?"* the response can be *"Because I said so. I'm in charge here until you become an adult."* Parents must make the final decisions.

Assign Chores

Before they can assume responsibility for their own lives, children must learn to be contributing members of a family. Chores teach basic living skills, enhance a child's feeling of worth, and provide a sense of accomplishment.

Teach Delayed Gratification

Stop trying to protect your children from frustration and defeat. Give regular doses of Vitamin N— standing for the character-building ingredient No.

Many of us have conditioned our children to a material standard beyond what we expect for ourselves. Giving children everything they ask for destroys the will to persist.

Crisis and conflict will be experienced by every family. The sooner children learn that life is difficult, the better they will learn to overcome frustration. Studies have shown that resolved crises bring families closer together. A good parent models the attitude, *"We will overcome this challenge and learn from it."*

Encourage Creativity

Introduce your children to clay, finger paints, building blocks and other toys that will enhance their creative urges. Creativity builds self-esteem. As children cultivate their talent their self-worth soars.

Turn off the Television.

Television-watching inhibits sequential thinking, motivation, curiosity, initiative, reasoning, and imagination. Watching television also shortens a child's attention span.

Numerous studies have shown a direct causal link between media violence and increased aggressiveness. Children who watch violent television programs demonstrate increased kicking and punching behavior when compared to children who watch nonviolent television programs.

Other than those things, television isn't bad. Educational programs, especially those that teach reading and social skills, can be encouraged—in moderation.

The maturing child can watch sports and entertainment programs if content and time are monitored.

Communication and Leadership

Discipline begins with good communication. Family meetings, held at least once weekly, improve communication by covering achievements, expectations, and responsibilities. Fun and a spirit of acceptance enhance productive meetings.

From these meetings and the examples their parents establish, children can learn self-discipline—the ability to fulfill one's needs in such a way that others are allowed to achieve their expectations. In teaching appropriate behavior use the following guidelines:

Communicate verbally and non-verbally that you want to help the child learn self-discipline.

Question inappropriate behavior.

Ask your child to evaluate his behavior.

Ask your child to give a plan that will more effectively enable him to get his needs met.

Ask your child to commit—with a handshake or written agreement—to the new alternative.

Give praise for good behavior. Praise solidifies involvement.

Use appropriate consequences as punishment. For example, no play until homework is done or no use of the car until it is washed.

Stick with the plan. Real changes in behavior take several months.

The Happy Home

No home is perfect—each one teaches vice and virtue. Our early home experiences, good or bad, become the moral compass that guides us for the rest of life's journey. Those homes that create an ambiance of good manners and simple justice will remain a cherished memory that promotes civilized behavior.

Here's a code for parents who seek to contribute to an enlightened world:

Catch your child doing something right and reward that behavior.

When your child makes a mistake, let the child know that you expect better.

Keep the lid on your temper when things go wrong. When you lose your temper you say things you regret later. Yelling, screaming, cursing are undignified and poor modeling. Anger is okay. Losing your temper is not.

Walk what you talk. Behave the way you want your children to behave.

Be consistent when making rules and bestowing punishment.

Keep your dignity. Don't dress, dance or talk like your kids.

Worship together.

Pray together.

Punish the behavior, love the child.

Don't be wishy-washy. Don't be intimidated by threats.

Be honest. Always tell the truth.

Summary

Parenthood is in itself an act of growing up.

When we learn the parenting lesson of the day, that particular challenge has passed and the next educational experience has begun.

We must learn to be firm but flexible; to give without expectation of return; to administer justice when we really just want to read the paper.

Being a good parent requires forgiveness and renewal, an excellent sense of humor, and attention to the basics of building strong family relationships. Here are some reminders:

Spend time with your children. Look at them. Listen to them. Read to them.

Hug them. Hold them. Cuddle them. You can never snuggle enough.

Speak what you want. Never speak what you don't want. Verbalize the positive.

Eat meals together.

Pray together.

Worship together.

Turn off the television.

Wherever you are...be there. Give full attention.

Give plenty of praise. Praising good behavior increases good behavior.

Avoid living your life through your children. Have your own life.

Have specific rules and regulations that everyone understands and agrees with.

Punish improper behavior by taking away privileges.

Encourage your children to participate in multiple activities. Let them take risks.

Keep your word. When you give a warning or make a promise, follow through.

Be flexible. Go with the flow. Laugh a lot. Remember: *"This too will pass."*

Walk the talk.

Tell the truth.

Admit your mistakes.

Time for Work

Love Made Visible

It is not enough to be busy ...
the question is: "What are we busy about?"
-- Henry David Thoreau

$\mathcal{W}$e work for three reasons:

1.　... to make money.
2.　... to productively use our talents.
3.　... to make a contribution to society.

Money is the prime mover for many of us. Some of us enjoy the pleasure of work more than the money our work brings. A few of us work to contribute to society—our work makes our love visible. A rare individual finds enjoyable work that combines all three motives and thus provides lifestyle.

This chapter is about developing lifestyle—making money, helping others, and having the time to enjoy the fruits of our labor.

Making Money

There are seven legal ways to acquire money:

Receive it as a gift or an inheritance.

Wager for it: win the lottery, gamble for it.

Have it work for you: invest money
tomake money.

Sell something for it.

Work for it: get a job or pursue a career.

Discover, invent, write, or produce something that earns a royalty or residual income.

Own a business.

Unfortunately, not all seven ways are equally available to each of us.

The vast majority of us don't have rich relatives.

The odds of winning the lottery: one in fifteen million.

You must have money to invest it: most of us don't.

Sales people have an excellent opportunity to make a lot of money: as long as they have the talent to sell and keep on selling.

Producing or making something is a great way to make money: if you have talent or if you have oil wells in your backyard.

Without a doubt the best and most reliable way to make money: own a business.

But before we get into owning a business, let's look at the traditional way of making money: *working for someone else.*

Characteristics of an Excellent Company

Excellent companies provide quality products that last, combined with service delivered promptly to customers who reign supreme. More specifically, the following seven features distinguish excellent companies:

- Customer satisfaction
- Respect for the individual

- Integrity
- Commitment to excellence
- Employee support and recognition
- Proper focus
- A willingness to change

Take this test to evaluate the standards at your company:

1. Do the people where you work feel good about themselves?

2. Does your company have strong leadership?

3. Is there adequate feedback on performance?

4. Does your company have a mission statement and goals to achieve that mission?

5. Do people where you work care about each other?

6. Does your company pay attention to detail?

7. Does your company seek new approaches?

8. Does your workplace have an atmosphere of enthusiasm and good will?

9. Does the customer come first where you work?

10. Does your company encourage individuals to develop their talents?

Here are some comments on these questions:

1. The more people like themselves, the better they perform.

   Several well-designed research studies have shown that 85% of success in business depends on people skills—*the ability to help people feel good about themselves*—and only 15% of success is related to technical skills.

   People skills are more than a friendly smile and a warm handshake.

The following five personality traits characterize those who can get the job done with people:

- Enthusiasm
- A *"can-do"* attitude
- Loyalty
- High energy level
- Assertiveness

2. Excellence comes from many directions, but usually from the top.

A good company needs a strong leader who likes action and results—a person who can make decisions quickly and clearly—a person who will delegate responsibility.

A good leader seeks and gives advice, listens carefully, and is attuned to employees' strengths and weaknesses.

3. Excellent companies provide feedback. When someone does a job well, their performance is noticed. And when someone has made a mistake, that person is shown how to perform the job correctly.

Behavior is criticized; the person is not. Along with feedback, excellent companies render appreciation—lot's of it—for those who deserve kudos. Appreciation is the best motivator.

Feedback, the breakfast of champion companies, encourages individual growth by providing each person with approval, appreciation, correction, and instruction.

4. The most successful companies know exactly what they are about. They have a brief, clear statement of purpose—to provide the most encouraging publications available—and specific goals aimed in that direction.

5. A good office environment has a family feeling. The people watch out for each other, celebrating individual and group successes and offering support where needed. They see themselves as a team with a common goal and they find that a supportive atmosphere makes them strong and efficient.

6. The best companies follow-up and follow-up can be found in the details of doing a job well. Telephone messages are delivered promptly. Numbers and facts are double-checked. Customers are called to check on their satisfaction. Follow-up tells a company how it's doing.

7. To survive in the competitive marketplace companies must be willing to change with the times. Excellent companies are always stretching. They look for newer and better approaches for doing things.

8. An enthusiastic greeting, happy employees and employers, a funny drawing, or sign that shows affection or humor gives the office an atmosphere of goodwill. A businesslike attitude is important, but let's not rule out fun and joy.

9. A company that doesn't respect the customer isn't going to last very long. And we would all do well to remember that employees are customers, too.

10. Companies that fail to encourage growth and development for their employees will lose their best people. Respect for the individual requires integrity marked by the following three rules:

   • do what's right.
   • do the best you can.
   • follow the Golden Rule: *treat others as you like to be treated.*

Efficient Meetings Save Time

Executives spend over ten hours a week in meetings–that's one-fourth of the work week. Most of this time is wasted. Here are some tips on making meetings work.

➨ Brevity–*in speech and in agenda*–encourages efficiency.

➨ Because meetings tend to expand to fill up the time allotted for them, wise leaders make certain that short—*very short*—meetings are scheduled.

➨ A meeting must involve crisp, clear, concise reporting.

➨ There should be a written, one sentence purpose for a meeting.

➨ Specific objectives for the meeting must be kept to one page.

➨ The leader must take control of the meeting.

➨ The leader should make a few brief opening remarks to set the tone of the meeting.

➨ Attendees must know the reason for their being present.

➨ The leader follows a specific agenda.

➨ A reporter should be appointed to condense the major points on a one page memo.

➨ The leader clarifies vague statements; confronts generalizations; and minimizes conflicts.

➨ If an important, but unplanned topic comes up, the leader delegates the study of the topic at a later date.

➨ The leader assertively wraps up each topic on time.

➨ At the meeting's conclusion points are summarized and work assignments given.

➨ Every meeting ends earlier than expected.

Bold Writing Saves Time

Writing concise letters and memos saves time and improves communication. Here are a few suggestions:

Write boldly. Bold writing saves time and space. To be brief, use the active voice. Instead of writing, *"There were a great number of memos lying on the floor,"* write, *"Memos covered the floor."* The active voice shortens and strengthens the sentence.

Make definite assertions. Expressing a negative in a positive form strengthens the sentence: *"dishonest"* is better than *"not honest"*; *"trifling"* is better than *"not important"*; *"forgot"* is better than *"did not remember."*

Use specific language. Good writers give details. Instead of *"A period of unfavorable re-engineering set in,"* write *"Fifty-one people lost their job last week."*

Omit needless words. Brevity commands attention. Change, *"He is a man who is tall"* to *"He is tall"*. Change, *"Owing to the fact that the bank was closed I had difficulty getting enough money,"* to *"Since the bank was closed I have no cash"*.

Be clear. When a sentence becomes muddled and difficulties with syntax arise, break up the sentence into two or more shorter sentences.

Concise language makes reading fun and conveys information clearly. ***Be bold. Be clear. Be brief. Save time. Make money.***

Owning a Business

Faced with insolvency (debt), inflation, and job insecurity, most of us work harder and longer than ever before. Four out of every ten Americans spend more than they make.

Our country circulates 800 million credit cards—an average of four cards for each man, woman and child in the United States. In 1994 we charged almost $500 billion on credit cards.

Inflation, the cruelest tax, destroys our economic security. The buying power of money is cut in half every ten to fifteen years depending on the inflation rate.

To find out how quickly your money decreases in value, use *"the rule of 72"* – divide the current rate of inflation into 72 to determine how many years it will take for your money to lose half of its buying power.

The one job family is disappearing. It takes two incomes—sometimes three and even four—for us to achieve the standard we seek.

The work situation has changed so rapidly that those who had what they once considered life-long positions have lost their jobs. Job security is an oxymoron. People are looking for alternatives.

Advantages of Owning a Business

Several benefits exist when you have a business of our own.

When you own a business you are the boss.
You have no one to blame for your failures and you can take credit for your successes. You can also go fishing anytime you feel like it, which, if you want to succeed is a poor idea–unless you own a fish market.

You have unlimited income potential. You can expand your company and your income. You will pay yourself what you are worth.

You have freedom. You make the decisions. No one else tells you *"what," "when," "where," "how,"* and *"why"* to do your job.

Problems With Owning A Business

Equally important are the several problems, and risks, you face when you have a business of our own.

An often prohibitive start-up cost.

A lack of knowledge. Especially if you have always worked for someone else, you may discover you lack certain knowledge or skills to run a business alone.

*The risk of owning a business frightens
many away.* 60% to 80% of new businesses
fail within five years.

Finally, there's time. Most of us don't have
enough time to start a business and continue
working at our regular job.

Multilevel Marketing Makes Time and Saves Money

The properly structured multilevel marketing business allows you to have the advantage of owning your
own business without prohibitive start-up costs. You can
continue with your present job and build your marketing business with your discretionary time.

If you choose the proper multilevel marketing company, you will get training from your friends and associates who sponsored you into the business. You can learn
from the mistakes and successes of those who proceeded
you.

Most legal multilevel marketing companies offer
low risk opportunities. If you choose the right company,
you will avoid risking large amounts of money on inventory requirements or training.

Of course, you must be careful when deciding about
any business venture. Don't get involved in anything
that promises quick money and no work. Anything of
value requires persistent and consistent work before a
big pay off. *Caveat emptor.*

Multilevel marketing companies generate time and
money. Here's how they work:

An individual pays a fee to join a company
that distributes a product or service.

*That individual buys the product from the
parent company* and receives a rebate check
from the company based on the amount pur-
chased.

The individual recruits others to join who in
turn recruit others who recruit others. Those who
join get a small percentage rebate for all the purchases made in their group.

"Win–Win" For Everyone Involved

Multilevel businesses, when organized properly, become *"Win–Win"* for everyone involved. Everybody has fun helping other people make money. The more people helped, the more money made.

A multilevel business multiplies time.

Pretend you joined a multilevel marketing company and spent five hours a week recruiting people to join.

Those you recruited also spent five hours weekly recruiting others who spent five hours, etc.

If your group grew to ten people-and each individual recruited five hours weekly-you would have fifty hours that counted for your business development.

And you only worked five hours a week!

Imagine having 100 people in your group ... ***your business would generate 500 hours a week that counted for you!***

The multilevel business never delivers that beautifully. People are people. Some are greedy. Some are lazy. Some are apathetic. Some are jerks.

Just as in any business, the 80/20 rule prevails.

And, of course, some multilevel companies cheat their recruits.

Nonetheless, a properly structured multilevel company provides the opportunity to multiply time and money.

Everyone can benefit from a safety net income. We all could use more money. We all need more time. Multilevel provides the best method for leveraging time. And making money-lots of it.

With money and the time to enjoy the money we make, we have given ourselves a balanced life ... *we have lifestyle.*

Characteristics of an Ideal Multilevel Company

Before you get involved with a multilevel company, do your homework. Here are the characteristics of an ideal multilevel company:

- The founders and officers of the company have an outstanding reputation.
- The company has a rock-solid financial base.
- The income projections and product performance claims are compatible with the company's official publications.
- The company offers a wide range of quality products and services.
- Start-up costs are low.
- Marketing information and demo materials are sold at company cost.
- The company commits to buy back starter kit, fees, and unsold inventory.
- There exists no inventory demand or minimum monthly purchase requirement.
- Distributor compensation is based on product and service movement.
- Personal retail sales are required to qualify for bonuses.
- No commissions or bonuses are paid to a sponsor for the mere act of recruiting.
- Training is given at no cost.
- The company's network provides a 100% money back guarantee on all products.
- The company demands no inventory purchases.
- The company has a record of paying their recruits' rebate checks on time.
- The company allows unlimited sponsoring opportunity.
- The company generates world wide distribution potential.

Summary

Whether we work for a company, own a business, or become involved in a multilevel opportunity, basic principles mandate success.

- The key to happiness involves finding work we enjoy and time to enjoy the money we make.
- Choice determines our happiness.
- Because we have the freedom to choose, we can choose to be happy.
- We can learn to be content in all things.

- Our occupations and the money we make matter very little in God's grand world.
- How we work does matter.

> *Whatever your hand finds to do,*
> *do it with all your might ....*
> -- Ecclesiastes 9:10

The joy we gain from our work is more important than the money we make.

Time for Fun

Laugh Out Loud – LOL

Work consists of whatever a body is obliged to do ...
Play consists of whatever a body is not obliged to do.
                                        -- Mark Twain

Since the publication of *An Anatomy of an Illness* by Norman Cousins in 1979, much has been written about the use of humor in achieving physical and emotional health.

Cousins, the former editor of *Saturday Review,* wrote about recovering from anklosing spondylitis, a rheumatoid-like disorder. Considering the hospital noisy and impersonal, Cousins checked into a hotel room where he read inspirational and humorous literature and watched Candid Camera and Groucho Marx film clips.

Although flat on his back with pain when the experiment began, within a few months Cousins returned to full-time work. He attributed his recovery to the cultivation of positive emotions. Humor used properly can be a beneficial antidote against anxiety, stress, tension and depression that contributes to physical illness.

Levels of Humor

Humor has three levels. Sarcasm—*hostile and destructive humor*—disparages relationships. If you say,

"I'd rather bring my wife to the convention than kiss her good-bye," you've interfered with an opportunity for romance. If your wife says, *"I've had 12 happy years of married life, which is not bad for 18 years of marriage,"* she reinforces a bad relationship.

Self-denigrating remarks as, *"I don't want to belong to a club that accepts people like me as members,"* reinforces a negative view of yourself. Claiming that your son, *"... would get into a fight in an empty room,"* establishes negative expectations. Avoid sarcasm and ridicule.

On the other hand *"belly-laugh"* humor reduces stress. When I was working on this chapter, I wrote a newspaper column about mistakes made while sending messages electronically on the computer, called as most of you know, e-mail. I pontificated grandly about how all of us who use the computer need to be careful. Several readers quickly informed me that my column contained a mistake, a huge one regarding computer language and abbreviations.

The mistake was so ludicrous that there was nothing I could do except laugh out loud and research computer short-hand so that I would not make the mistake again. During my investigation I discovered a plethora of e-mail abbreviations including the one used as a subtitle for this chapter–LOL.

LOL stands for ***"Laugh Out Loud."*** LOL is in, *"belly laugh"* is out.

Jokes cause us to LOL in one of three ways:

- Overstating the truth
- Understating the truth
- Producing incongruity–ending in surprise.

Here are two examples of overstated humor:

"What's the fastest way to become a Texas oil millionaire? Start out as a Texas billionaire."

"What's the difference between the Titanic and the oil business? The Titanic had a band."

Mark Twain was a master of understated humor: *"The efficiency of our jury system is only marred by the difficulty of finding 12 men every day who don't know anything and can't read."*

Lou Holtz gives us a good example of incongruity. When coaching for the University of Minnesota he said, *"Minnesota is a great state with beautiful kids. They all have blond hair and blue ears."*

Here's another example of incongruity. Humorist Robert Benchley walked out of the Ritz Hotel and beckoned to a man who wore epaulets on his shoulders. Benchley, assuming the man was a doorman, asked him to call a cab. The man replied, *"I'll have you know, sir, I'm an Admiral in the United States Navy."* Benchley retorted, *"Well, call us a battleship then."*

The highest level of humor, cosmic humor, allows us to appreciate the absurdities and the paradoxes of life. Viewing our frustrations with humor—learning to laugh at ourselves and our problems—allows us to be more flexible and better balanced.

Or, as Will Rogers said, *"Friends, I don't give advice. But, if I did, I'd just say that we're only on this earth for a short time; so for Heaven's sake have a few laughs and don't take things so seriously, especially ourselves. Just live your life so you wouldn't be ashamed to sell the family parrot to the town gossip."*

If You Can't LOL–Smile

Smiling behavior–turning our lips in an upward direction–makes us feel better.

Neurobiologists hypothesize that using the facial muscles to smile cuts off the circulation in the carotid artery (the vessel in the neck that supplies blood to the brain). This decrease in blood circulation impacts on the limbic area of the brain that influences the pituitary which in turn stimulates the hypothalamus and endorphins are secreted.

This explanation, a terrible over simplification that would get me kicked out of the Neurobiology Association (if I were a member), indicates that smiling may cause a release of the central nervous system euphorogenic, endorphin–and that's why we feel better when we smile.

Whatever the explanation, smiling improves our looks and our out look. So smile–*it makes life a whole lot better.*

Humor Tips

Have you ever noticed how people on the tennis court or the golf course shout and act as if they are fighting alligators in a swamp. If they aren't having a terrible time, they're certainly making life miserable for everybody around them. Those who enjoy life, play for the fun of playing. Paradoxically, when they're playing for the fun, they play better.

The next time you're playing golf and someone asks for your handicap tell them, *"I'm blind in the left eye and deaf."* Or, *"I play military golf: Left, right, left, right."*

Remember, *enjoy*. And follow these suggestions:

- Decide to be hopeful and fun-loving.
- Every day ask yourself, *"Am I having fun yet?"*
- Surround yourself with people who fill you with joy and laughter.
- Be an inverse paranoid-think the world is out to do you good.
- When a situation becomes stressful, pretend it's all a Candid Camera episode.
- Read or listen to humor regularly.
- Keep a humor scrapbook.
- Marry someone who thinks everything you say is funny.
- Understand that few things are absolute or sacred—even Ann Landers got a divorce.
- Don't take yourself so seriously.
- Remember: *He who laughs, lasts.*
- Practice LOL–it's internal jogging.
- Play golf. Golf is just like life: Difficult and unfair. Par is 18 laughs a round.

Developing A Humorous Lifestyle

Those people who have a cosmic view of life cultivate a lifestyle that allows them to tolerate outrageous fortune. They don't take things so seriously. They laugh at themselves and their situations. They develop a *"hang-loose"* philosophy of life.

For example, Satchel Paige, the great, black baseball pitcher, didn't get to toss a curve ball in the Major Leagues until he was 42. Paige, who may have been the best pitcher ever to throw a baseball, spent most of his career in the old Negro Leagues, but he was able to tolerate rejection because of his humorous approach to life.

Here are his six rules for living:

1. Avoid fried meats which angry up the blood.

2. If your stomach disputes you, lie down and pacify it with cool thoughts.

3. Keep the juices flowing by jangling around gently as you move.

4. Go very lightly on the vices, such as carrying on in society. The social ramble ain't restful.

5. Avoid running at all times.

6. Don't look back. Something might be gaining on you.

Friendship

Those who enjoy life develop their abilities while earning the goodwill and respect of others. They incite gratitude, humor, and happiness and give without demands.

Those who win friends demonstrate the following traits:

- They have a genuine interest in others.
- They encourage others to talk about themselves.
- They show respect for the other person's opinion.
- They spread joy, enthusiasm, and good will.
- They share their feelings openly and honestly.
- They have a nonjudgmental, uncritical attitude.
- They know how to laugh and have fun.

Play and Leisure

Play—free and spontaneous activity—emphasizes enjoyment not achievement. Emotion, not effort, enhances play.

Here are some suggestions and thoughts on having fun:

- Quit work early or take time off when fatigue builds.

- Plan an occasional long weekend away from work.
- Schedule vacations and keep them.
- Attitude, not activity, determines whether we work or play.
- Sustained effort toward a goal is best balanced with laughter and play.
- Leisure activity should be fun, not a drain on the emotions.
- Returning to work tired after a vacation indicates the wrong approach to leisure time.
- Sports and games should bring more laughs than frowns.
- The one beat per second timing of Baroque music (Bach, Handel, Vivaldi) helps relax the mind and enhances learning.
- Learning something new—acting, painting, playing a musical instrument—stimulates child-like fun and creativity.
- Pet owners always have a friend.
- Hobbies prevent boredom.
- Reading provides a life of constant renewal.

Cultivating Creativity

Creative people see connections between things when others see separation. How does one learn to be creative?

First, creativity requires knowledge, for many creative ideas come from old concepts rearranged in a new way. Knowledge alone, of course, won't make us creative. The more we know, however, the more flexible we can be in our thinking and the more we'll be able to turn things upside-down and inside-out.

Gutenberg, for example, combined two previously unconnected ideas, the wine press and the coin punch, to create the printing press. A creative marketing person labeled *Seven-Up*™ the un-cola. creating an alternative to dozens of colas on the market. Picasso took the seat and handlebars of a bicycle, welded them together and created the head of a bull. Nolan Bushness, bored by watching television, got it to respond to him, creating *Pong*, the first video game.

Here are some suggestions to stimulate creativity:

- Look for a second right answer. Keep looking for different approaches and alternatives to the old way of doing things.
- Try to see similarities among things—a river is like life, for example, with many twists and turns, smooth places and rough.
- Break the rules by questioning the reasoning behind them. Alexander untied the *Gordian Knot* by chopping it in half while others had failed for centuries because they followed the rule and tried to untie it.
- Ask *"what if"* questions. Einstein conceived the theory of relativity by asking, *"What if I could ride a light beam?"*
- Think ambiguously. Heraclitus said, *"Harmony consists of opposing tension."* If engineers had read Heraclitus they might have constructed the Brooklyn Bridge sooner.
- Make mistakes. Errors indicate you're trying something new. If you don't make a mistake from time to time, you won't achieve anything new—and you'll be so boring.

Summary

A film lover's classic, *Sullivan's Travels,* tells the story of a movie producer who decides to become a hobo so he can understand the *"common people."*

Through a series of misadventures the producer ends up in a chain gang. One night he and his fellow prisoners watch a movie, a comedy. As the inmates laugh away their trouble, the producer realizes that helping people see humor in daily events provides hope for us all.

A sense of humor—that goes beyond joke telling—embraces laughing at oneself and life's absurdities. When we learn to *"think funny"* our life becomes enriched with friends and fellowship.

Time for Spirit

Losing Life to Gain Life

*What good will it be for a man
if he gains the whole world, yet forfeits his soul?*
-- Matthew 16:26

*L*iving an abundant life requires that we take time to enjoy God.

Communicating with God demands disciplined concentration. Through scriptural study, meditation, and prayer we become aware of the still, soft voice within. This gentle whisper heard in the quietness of a humbled heart awakens us to those experiences that enrich the soul.

The Word of God

The Holy Bible, more than a collection of stories, is the inspired word of God. God revealed, through the Holy Spirit, His person and plan to believers who wrote down His message in the context of their own cultural, historical, and personal experiences. They used their own style, language, and minds to write what God wanted them to write.

Because the entire Holy Bible is God's inspired word we can use it to guide our lives. Useful in teaching and correcting us, the Bible is the standard for testing all other knowledge. All of us would do well to set aside time everyday to read God's holy word so that we can live a life of confidence and faith. (My wife, Victoria, and I, to start our day right, read the scriptures in the morning.) Through scriptural study and prayer we can better glorify God and enjoy Him forever.

Thoughts on Prayer

Prayer is unlike putting a nickel in a gum machine, twisting a handle, and then waiting for the gum to pop out. Asking God for a yellow bicycle is similar to mailing a list of Christmas wishes to the North Pole.

God is not Santa Claus and treating God as if He were cheats us out of the treasured relationship we can have with Him.

Prayer is not a numbers game. Notre Dame's football victory over Southern Methodist University has nothing to do with who has the most people praying for success. Notre Dame wins because their players are bigger, stronger, and faster. (Winning coaches pray like God decides victories and they recruit like He doesn't.)

Can we receive what we ask in prayer? Yes. But a relationship with God comes first. To have the abundant life God desires for us, requires that we take time to experience His power. Prayer allows us to develop a proper relationship with God that enables us to live the life He wants for us.

As we gradually, progressively develop a deep, abiding commitment to God, we feel His presence in all that we do. When we begin to pray as He wants us to pray— when we become aligned with His will—He begins to answer our prayers.

A relationship with God requires discipline. We begin by praying mechanically, and, with time, we can learn to communicate with God at deeper levels. God meets us where we are and gradually moves us toward a holy life.

Here, then, are some rudimentary suggestions on developing the habit of daily prayer.

- Set aside a particular time each day for prayer.
- Openness, honesty and trust mark good communication with God.

- Pray simply.
- Pray hopefully.
- Pray constantly—waiting in line, waiting for a traffic light to change, visiting your children as they sleep.
- Pray for others. Pray for your loved ones, but pray also for your enemies and your provocateurs.
- Take time to listen. Passive prayer builds a powerful relationship with God.

While learning to pray, it's probably best to stick with the same regimen. In time, prayers will become more spontaneous, but they will ordinarily focus on the following topics:

Thanksgiving. Thank God for all you have been given. Recount your abundance:

- Health
- Friends
- Loved Ones
- Home
- Work

  —*all that is good in life.*

Others. Pray for your family members to be surrounded by the peace and warmth of God's love. Pray for friends and associates who are in need. Ask for help in understanding adversaries.

Virtues. Ask God for love, joy, peace of mind, wisdom, courage, patience, humility and faith.

Goals. Ask God for the strength and dedication to help fulfill His purpose for you.

Confession. Admit your mistakes, errors, and sins. Yes, contrary to popular wishes, sin exists. We all sin—everyday. Anything that separates us from God's love is sin. When we put our lives, our careers, our wishes above God, we sin. But—good news—God forgives us when we confess. Confession frees our spirit to follow God's will for our lives.

Forgiveness. Ask God to forgive your shortcomings and ask for help in forgiving those who have offended you.

The Abundant Life

Helen Keller, in her wonderful essay, *Three Days To See*, wrote touchingly on those things she would choose to look upon if granted a brief gift of sight. Keller, struck blind, deaf and mute in infancy, lived a remarkable life. In the face of unimaginable difficulty, she came to understand the true value of living.

My daughter, Wende, in freshman English class, received an assignment to read Keller's essay and then write what she would do if she had only three days of sight. Her essay was so beautifully written and deeply considered that I would like to share her thoughts with you.

If she had three days to see, Wende wrote, she wouldn't spend them visiting exotic places. Instead, she would take a long morning to browse through the family photo albums, implanting in her mind's eye the beautiful memories of growing up. Then she would look, really look, at her brother, focusing in on his childlike innocence, his wonderful naiveté. She would visit a newborn nursery and be reminded by mother and child that when we love another person we see the face of God.

The next morning she would spend with her parents. She wanted to remember my warm smile and she would make certain at last to appreciate my breakfast cheer and enthusiasm. She would be filled with wonder for the last time as she saw in her mother's eyes the expression of those qualities she admired—strength of character, purpose, and integrity.

Part of that day she would spend with her boyfriend, appreciating his healthy good looks, the way he moved, his sudden grin. Then Wende would gaze into the mirror at her reflected image. This time she would look for the things she liked about her face and body instead of concentrating on the flaws.

On the third day she would drive through the countryside. Coming upon a field of flowers, she would appreciate them from afar and then study them at close range because we don't really understand something until it is viewed close-up and from a distance. Sometimes pulling back from things allows us to better understand their substance. Sometimes we need to get closer.

As the day turned to night, Wende would step outside and take in the stars—a permanent reminder of the vastness of the universe and the great mysteries that, in time, will be understood. She would spend her final hour gazing at those stars, meditating on the goodness of life. As her eyesight faded, visual memories would remain implanted in her mind—memories that would continue to enrich her life throughout her years.

Wende's essay reminds us of the importance of fully experiencing each moment of each day. In the poignant third act of Thornton Wilder's play, *Our Town*, Emily dies but is allowed by God to return to life for one day.

Choosing to live the moments of her twelfth birthday, Emily experiences the family too busy to pay attention to each other.

Emily, alone in the center of the stage, says, *"Oh! Oh! It goes so fast. We don't have time to look at one another."* She asks, *"Do any human beings ever realize life while they live it—every, every minute? That's all human beings are! Just blind people."*

The psalmist observed, *"Eyes have they, but they see not."* Let's resolve to make time each day to look, really look, at the people and things we love. Let's view our problems close up and then step back and get a different perspective. Time spent paying attention, contemplating, and being thankful allows us to see, really see.

In the Lerner and Lowe musical, *Camelot*, King Arthur is preparing to battle his best friend, Lancelot, who has betrayed him. His life's love, Guinevere, has been banned to a convent. Arthur feels that all he had worked for—justice and peace—had been lost.

Sitting on a hillside in France, contemplating his despair, Arthur hears rustling in the nearby woods. He calls out and a small boy, Thomas, appears. Arthur asks Thomas what he wants. Thomas replies that he wants to fight for the knights of the round table. He wants to keep Camelot's flame burning.

Admonishing Thomas to run behind the lines, Arthur sends the boy back to England to tell and keep alive the story, *"That once there was a fleeting wisp of glory known as Camelot."* Arthur's companion appears and asks, *"Who was that boy?"* Arthur replies, *"Just a tiny drop in the great blue ocean of the sunlit sea–but some of the drops do sparkle. Some of the drops do sparkle."*

When we turn our life over to God—when we lose our life to God's will–we gain our life. Our love, our work, and our joy become complete when we devote our lives to God. We begin, then, to see our life as a tiny drop in the great blue ocean of the sunlit sea—a tiny blue drop that sparkles. We possess the abundant life.

Summary

God is a powerful, loving force all around and within us. Daily prayer is both a humbling and a spiritually uplifting discipline that allows love, peace of mind and joy to permeate our lives and the lives of others. As we become more aware of our spiritual essence through prayer, meditation, and study of the scriptures we can use additional methods and ideas to assist in our continued spiritual growth:

- Discover the sources of fulfillment within you.

- Accept your own mortality.

- Read what others have discovered about spiritual growth.

- Strengthen your religious ties.

- Be generous with love.

- Remain ever on the lookout for new experiences that can enrich your soul and teach you more about life.

Time for Reading

Of Making Many Books There Is No End

Our lives change in two ways:
through the people we meet and the books we read
-- Harvey Mackay

*t*he people of Springfield, Illinois little realized what destiny held for Abraham Lincoln.

Most pitied him. Married to a virago who embarrassed him with her envious, hostile outbursts, he withstood twenty-two years of her verbal abuse. His ill-fitting clothes often had buttons missing and always needed pressing. Until the day he left for Washington, he milked his cow, groomed his horse, and cut his own firewood. Cash short, he borrowed money from friends for his Presidential inauguration trip.

His past failure bode poorly for future success. Beset by business insolvency twice, he spent 17 years paying off his debt; he suffered a nervous breakdown after the love of his life, Ann Rutledge, died; and lost eight elections—state legislature, speaker of the state legislature, elector, US Congress (twice defeated), land officer, US Senate (twice defeated), and a vice-presidential nomination.

Most of the people opposed Lincoln most of the time. Even his relatives voted against him! When he ran for President, only one cousin on his mother's side, and none on his father's side, cast a ballot for him. Twenty of the twenty-three ministers in his hometown opposed him. Lincoln became President because the three candidates in the election split the vote allowing Lincoln to enter office backed by less than a majority of voters.

General McClellan, the commander of the Army of the Potomac, constantly insulted the President that appointed him. Once when Lincoln visited him, McClellan kept him waiting for half an hour. On another occasion, informed that Lincoln had been waiting for hours to see him, McClellan crept to his bedroom and sent word that he had gone to bed.

Almost every man in the Cabinet considered himself superior to Lincoln. Salmon P. Chase, Secretary of the Treasury, shocked at Lincoln's country ways, criticized him ceaselessly. Edward M. Stanton called Lincoln *"a painful imbecile"* and *"the original gorilla."*

How could Lincoln withstand defeat after defeat, criticism heaped upon criticism? How could he rise above his social limitations to become one of the greatest leaders the world has known? Answer—Reading.

Lincoln read the proper books. He filled his mind and soul with wisdom from the ages. Except for God's spirit in his life, there can be no other explanation for Lincoln's strength of character. His father was a ne'er-do-well; his mother died when he was nine; his childhood was marked by neglect and deprivation.

But Lincoln read. He read the Bible and Aesop's *Fables* so often that they affected his manner of talking and his method of thinking. He wore out a borrowed copy of the *Life of Washington*. Perhaps his richest find was Scott's *Lessons* containing speeches of Cicero, Demosthenes and Shakespeare's characters. He studied the book until he could recite long poems and speeches by heart.

Lincoln devoured books throughout his life. Biographies. Humor. History. Law. During the Civil War, Lincoln spent hours reading. Many times he would read passages from Shakespeare to his Cabinet, personal secretary, and visiting dignitaries and friends. Yes, more than any other factor, the books Lincoln read molded his character and enabled him to withstand the agony of outrageous fortune.

During his debates with Douglas Lincoln said,

"I am not bound to win, but I am bound to be true.

"I am not bound to succeed, but I am bound to live up to the light I have."

Rather than founding his self-worth on the opinions of others, Lincoln lived by an internal light,

... an internal light implanted by enduring character traits formulated by reading.

Here, then, are some books that will enable us to live up to the light we have been given:

The Relaxation Response, Herbert Benson, M.D.
How I Raised Myself from Failure to Success in Selling, Frank Bettger
The One Minute Manager, Kenneth Blanchard, Ph.D., and Spencer Johnson, M.D.
The Holistic Way to Health and Happiness, Harold Bloomfield, M.D., and Robert Kory, Ph.D.
The New Mood Therapy, David D. Burns, M.D.
The Tongue–The Creative Force, Charles Capps
How To Stop Worrying and Start Living, Dale Carnegie
How To Win Friends and Influence People, Dale Carnegie
Lincoln the Unknown, Dale Carnegie
An Anatomy of an Illness, Norman Cousins
Life on the Edge, James C. Dobson, Ph.D.
Healing Words, Larry Dossey, M.D.
Reality Therapy, William Glasser, M.D.
What You Say Is What You Get, Don Gossett
Just as I Am, Billy Graham
Who Stole the American Dream? Burke Hedges
You Can't Steal Second with Your Foot on First, Burke Hedges
Network of Champions, Shad Helmstetter, Ph.D.
What Do You Say When You Talk to Yourself? Shad Helmstetter, Ph.D.
The Master Key to Riches, Napoleon Hill
Think and Grow Rich, Napoleon Hill
Success, Michael Korda

When All You've Had Isn't Enough, Rabbi Harold
    Kushner,
How To Get Control of Your Life and Time, Alan
    Lakein, Ph.D.
Mere Christianity, C. S. Lewis
On the Anvil, Max Lucado
Psycho-cybernetics, Maxwell Maltz, M.D.
The Greatest Salesman in the World, Og Mandino
Hung By the Tongue, Francis Martin
Be a People Person, John Maxwell
Developing the Leaders Around You, John Maxwell
Developing the Leader Within You, John Maxwell
The Winning Attitude, John Maxwell
Bringing Out the Best in People, Alan Loy McGinnis
Happiness is a Choice, Frank B. Minirth, Ph.D.,and
    Paul D. Meier, M.D.
*The Complete Guide to Your Emotions and Your
    Health,* Emrika Padus
The Power of Positive Thinking, Norman Vincent
    Peale
People of the Lie, Scott Peck, M.D.
The Road Less Traveled, Scott Peck, M.D.
In Search of Excellence, Thomas J. Peters and
    Robert H. Waterman
How Faith Works, Frederick Price
The Magic of Thinking Big, David Schwartz, Ph.D.
Stress Without Distress, Hans Selye, M.D.
Improving Your Serve, Charles R. Swindol
The Elements of Style, William Strunk, Ph.D. and
    E.B. White
New Testament Commentary, John Wesley
See You at the Top, Zig Ziglar

Two of my early books may also be of interest:
    A Life Well Lived and *Fifty Ways to Keep Your
    Lover*, John Ingram Walker, M.D.

Summary

As I worked on this bibliography, I
began adding an extensive list of my favorite
books but because I ran out of space the recommendations are limited to those I used
in writing *Leverage Your Time, Balance
Your Life.*

Time, Balance Your Life.

As was true of Lincoln, my two favorite books are *The Holy Bible* and *The Complete Works of Shakespeare.* I read from those a little each day and suggest that you would benefit from the same plan.

I enjoy and recommend biographies of the famous and the infamous to inspire and to warn.

The Lifetime Reading Plan by Clifton Fadiman and *How to Read a Book* by Mortimer J. Adler and Charles Van Doren can be used as starters to a cultured education.

John Ingram Walker, M.D.

Dr. Walker is Medical Director for Professional and Community Education of Laurel Ridge Hospital, San Antonio, Texas and President, Life Works Publishing Company, a multimedia publisher focusing on quality of life issues and how to thrive in an era of industrial change.

At Duke University Medical Center, Durham, NC, Dr. Walker was Director, Combined Medical Specialties Unit and later served as Clinical Professor of Psychiatry at the University of Texas Health Science Center, San Antonio, Texas.

In addition to *Leverage Your Time, Balance Your Life*, Dr. Walker has authored seven books and edited four. He has also published more than 150 articles and book chapters. His best selling Nightingale-Conant audio-cassette, *Total Self-Help*, is the gold standard guide for personal growth.

A member of the National Speaker's Association, Dr. Walker has presented over 500 lectures nationwide and presented employee training and motivation programs for more than 25 corporations and professional associations including: 3M, Consumer Value Stores (CVS), H-E-B Food Stores, Hilton Hotels, Wyndham Hotels, Smith Barney, Upjohn, Internal Revenue Service, Methodist Hospital System, HARCO Pharmaceuticals, Structural Metals, Inc, West Point Pepperell, Wal-Mart, National Petroleum Management Association and the U.S. Armed Services Command.

My mission

To bring encouragement, inspiration, and hope to all I meet.

Specifically I'd like to make you laugh a little, think some, appreciate more, and, perhaps, on rare occasions, shed a tear or two.

I want you to know that Life Works.